"... This book serves as a patent "Bible" for all levels of inventors decorated with excellent examples covering all possible areas of invention.... It is obvious that the author combined a wide scientific background with the deep knowledge of patent law to create for us a dictionary for protecting ideas."
—ALISA BUCHMAN, *Senior Researcher and Group Leader, Technion-Israel Institute of Technology, Haifa, Israel*

"... This book will make a very good reference tool for anyone involved in the generation or protection of intellectual property."
—MATTHEW S. GOODWIN, *Senior Patent Attorney, Johnson & Johnson, New Brunswick, New Jersey*

"This is the book for individual inventors, research scientists, university professors, and corporate executives looking to patent new ideas or inventions.... Joy Bryant tells it 'like it really is' in the patent world with advice founded on a solid background of experience. She offers a step by step description of the 'who, what, when, where, and how' approach to anyone thinking of patenting a product or idea.... From the layman to the top executive, this easy reading book will enlighten you and lay out the steps necessary to protect your invention or idea.... A 'must have' item in any business library."
—JOSEPH T. ANTONUCCI, *President & CEO, Skylab Technologies Group, Inc., Jacksonville, Florida*

"Anyone who has ever had an inspired idea should read this book.... From students to researchers to corporate executives, simple advice and easy-to-follow guidance that can save time, money, and resources can be found in this straightforward reference/manual."
—DIANE M. FLYNN, *Founder & President, Flynn Consulting, London, England*

"Joy Bryant makes the patent system seem approachable, in a meaningful way, for the inventors it is meant to serve. Her enthusiasm for patents is contagious."
—ANTHONY P. VENTURINO, ESQ., P.E., *Partner, Stevens, Davis, Miller & Mosher, L.L.P., Washington, DC*

"Joy Bryant has presented a wonderful overview of patent fundamentals and the patenting process, in an easy-to-read format that can be used by anyone from an individual inventor to a professional patent practitioner. This book is a valuable addition to any patent reference library!"

—VIVIEN TSANG, *Patent Attorney,*
The Sherwin-Williams Company, Cleveland, Ohio

"This is a lucid and comprehensive exposition of what any inventor needs to know about the patenting process. Reading this book is more than likely to result in better quality patents, less post-issue problems, and will save the inventor(s) time and money for tutoring by a patent professional."

—TED KOHN, *Director, Patenting and Licensing, Virginia Tech*
Intellectual Properties, Inc., Blacksburg, Virginia

"If you have an idea and think it has commercial potential, read this book before talking to anyone. It could be worth millions."

—JOHN M. BACON, *Business Development Specialist, MidAtlantic*
Technology Applications Center, Pittsburgh, Pennsylvania

". . . No single source of information relating to intellectual property does so good a job as Joy Bryant's book in making the already complex world of the inventor less complicated by serving as the definitive source of information on copyrights, patents, and trademarks. I would recommend this book to the basement inventor, the faculty researcher, and the Fortune 500 research manager alike."

—TED D. ZOLLER, *Director of Economic Development,*
College of William & Mary, Williamsburg, Virginia

". . . The author's treatment of the subject eliminates much of the mystery surrounding the patent process and provides a guide which can greatly assist individuals who work in an academic environment where intellectual property is becoming an increasingly important component of the public research endeavor, but who are not themselves experts in the patent process."

—JANE LOPEZ, *Director, Sponsored Programs,*
Virginia Institute of Marine Science, Gloucester Point, Virginia

PROTECTING YOUR
IDEAS

The Inventor's Guide to Patents

PROTECTING YOUR
IDEAS

The Inventor's Guide to Patents

Joy L. Bryant

ACADEMIC PRESS

San Diego   London   Boston   New York   Sydney   Tokyo   Toronto

Reader's Responsibility when Using This Guide

Academic Press has done its best to ensure the accuracy of the information presented
in this book as of the publication date. The purpose of this book is to provide the
reader with general information about the subject matter presented for working in
concert with a registered patent practitioner. Hence, this book is not intended as,
nor should you consider it as, legal advice applicable to your specific situation.
Laws are frequently updated, and are often subject to differing interpretations.
You are solely responsible for your use of this book. Neither Academic Press
nor the author will be responsible to you or anyone else because of any information
contained in or left out of this book.

Academic Press
a division of Harcourt Brace & Company
525 B Street, Suite 1900, San Diego, California 92101-4495, USA
http://www.apnet.com

Academic Press
24-28 Oval Road, London NW1 7DX, UK
http://www.hbuk.co.uk/ap/

Library of Congress Catalog Card Number: 98-86601

International Standard Book Number: 0-12-138410-1

PRINTED IN THE UNITED STATES OF AMERICA
98 99 00 01 02 03 ML 9 8 7 6 5 4 3 2 1

This book is dedicated
to the memory of
Stephen Cooper,
known to and
remembered by many
as the
"technology prophet."

Contents

1

Choose the Right Protection

2

The Types of Patents and Patent Applications

3

The Invention Process

4

Documenting Your Ideas

8

Filing and Prosecuting the Patent Application

9

Deciding to Patent

Appendix

Appendix

Appendix **III**

Appendix

Preface

Have you ever had a good idea but were not sure how to protect it? If so, then this book was written for you. It will serve as an informative guide describing the types of intellectual property and, more specifically, patents and the patent process. What this book will not do is teach you how to prepare and file your own patent application. To do so would be a mistake. After all, would you want to risk a possible multimillion-dollar judgment based on a document that you have written—much less a document in an area of law you know little or nothing about? Patent law is complex and constantly changing. In fact, it is so specialized that many attorneys cannot practice patent law. Writing a patent application is a blend of technical and legal writing that requires an understanding of science and the law.

By the time you have finished reading this book, you will have a general understanding of copyrights, trademarks, trade secrets, patents, and the patent process. In addition, defined for you are your roles and responsibilities in the patent process when working with a patent practitioner. First, you must realize that not all ideas qualify as patentable subject matter. Therefore, in Chapter 1, you are presented with a general overview of intellectual property and its importance. In addition, this chapter helps you decide what form(s) of intellectual property will protect your idea by describing the types of intellectual property protection and the coverage each one offers. Chapter 2 introduces you to the types of patents. What you may not know is that (1) there are several kinds of patents and (2) not only do they protect specific types of inventions, but they are enforceable for different lengths of time. Chapter 3 introduces you to the legal definitions of the invention process and its application in the United States, which is *not* a first to file country. Chapter 4 stresses the importance of documenting your ideas. Documentation is perhaps the most important thing you can do to protect your inventions before they are patented. Chapter 5 discusses how to research your idea. Conducting a literature search before constructing your invention will save you much time and money in the long run. Chapter 6 teaches you how to protect yourself from yourself. In particular, this chapter introduces you to all the things that either you or someone else may do that would prevent you from getting a patent. Many people have come to me when it is too late to protect their inventions. Had they known the information in Chapter 6, they could have protected their ideas. Chapter 7 focuses on preparing the patent application with the help of a patent practitioner. In particular, it is designed to help you understand the value that the patent practitioner adds and what the patent practitioner needs to prepare a good application for you. Chapter 8 introduces you to the patent filing and prosecution process from the inventor's side of the desk. This chapter outlines the various papers the inventor is required to sign when submitting a patent application, as well as outlining the patent prosecution process. Chapter 9 gives you some information to consider before you decide to enter the patent process. Not all inventions should be patented. However, patenting is the only way you will be able to exclude others from making, using, selling, offering to sell, or importing your invention in the United States.

This book also contains several appendices. Appendix I provides a table of resources and contact information to find the help that you will need when you decide to protect your intellectual property. Appendix II lists the patent and trademark depository libraries found throughout the United States. Appendix III provides some important tips regarding invention development firms. Finally, Appendix IV is a checklist of what you need to have with you before you see your patent practitioner.

The ultimate goal of this book is to provide you with the information you need to:

1. make a wise decision about protecting your intellectual property;
2. work well with your patent practitioner; and
3. obtain the best possible protection for your ideas.

Acknowledgment

I thank the many people who contributed comments and criticism to help shape this book and shape my life as a professional:

Dr. Robert G. Bryant, Senior Chemical Engineer, NASA Langley Research Center, for his careful review of each chapter and its design. Rob provided the inventor's perspective for the book and guidance in the arrangement of the chapter content. Also, I thank Rob as my husband for the love, encouragement, and support that he provided me so this book would be completed on time.

Walter E. Crosmer, Section Head, Honeywell, Inc., for providing an industrial perspective for the book. Walt's critical review of each chapter helped ensure that the book would apply to the industrial inventor. (Thanks, Dad!)

Anne Womack, Director of Sponsored Programs, The College of William and Mary, for serving as a sounding board and providing the academic perspective when reviewing each chapter.

Debbie G. Ramos, neighbor and friend, for helping me keep the writing simplistic and clear.

Dr. Frank J. Cynar, Acquisitions Editor, Academic Press, for the many brainstorming sessions and for his guidance throughout each chapter.

Additional appreciation goes to the members of the National Association of Patent Practitioners who, unknowingly, contributed to this book by answering many of my questions on their list serve. I especially acknowledge the following members who donated their time to review and criticize various chapters, ensuring that the facts were correct:

Dr. Cheryl H. Agris, Esq., Registered Patent Attorney, formerly of Novo Nordisk, currently in private practice, Pelham, New York, for her careful review of Chapters 3–8. Cheryl went above and beyond the call of duty and was there for me when I needed her most.

Chester T. Barry, Esq., Registered Patent Attorney with Shanks & Herbert, Alexandria, Virginia, for his review of Chapter 1. Chester's knowledge of intellectual property law was a tremendous help to me in clarifying those areas of intellectual property law I do not practice.

Dr. Frederick L. Herman, Registered Patent Agent, Johnson & Johnson, for his review of Chapter 2. Fred's knowledge about foreign filing and PCT practice was helpful in clarifying such complex processes.

Michael F. Allan, Licensing Executive, First Principals, Inc., for his guidance on Chapter 9. Mike provided much insight into and information on the licensing and technology transfer process.

Last, I express my appreciation to my clients and the many inventors who have called me with questions. These questions helped me recognize the need for this book and motivated me to write it in the first place. I encourage these people to continue inventing and protecting their inventions with patents.

1

Choose the Right Protection

The first step in protecting an idea is to identify what type of protection you need. This is accomplished by gaining an understanding of what intellectual property encompasses.

What Is Meant by the Term "Intellectual Property"?

Ideas such as expressions, inventions, unique names, business methods, industrial processes, and chemical formulas are products of the mind. When these "products" are treated as property or given the legal aspects of property-type protection, they become intellectual property.

Intellectual property is a product of the mind treated as if it were a piece of property. Intellectual property is a collective term identifying copyrights, trademarks, trade secrets, patents, unfair competition, moral rights, and the right of publicity.

At least one form of intellectual property may protect each product of the mind. In turn, this protection makes it possible for a product of the mind to be owned, commercially exploited, and enforced by the courts. This chapter addresses the origins and use of copyrights, trademarks, trade secrets, and patents that protect various ideas.

What Are Copyrights, Trademarks, Trade Secrets, and Patents?

A **copyright** is a federal right, providing the author of an original work or the owner of the copyright the right to exclude others from:

(1) reproducing the work;

(2) preparing derivative works based on the original work;

(3) distributing the work to the public;

(4) performing the work in public;

(5) displaying the work in public; and

(6) for sound recordings, performing the work in public through digital audio transmission.[1]

A **trademark** is any word, name, symbol, or device, or any combination of words, names, symbols, and/or devices that identifies and distinguishes one's goods from those manufactured or sold by others. A trademark also indicates the source of goods, even if that source is unknown.[2]

A **trade secret** protects all forms and types of confidential business information if: (a) the owner has taken reasonable measures to keep such information secret; and (b) the information derives independent economic value, actual or potential, from not being generally known to, and not being readily found out through proper means by the public.[3]

A **U.S. patent** is an agreement between an inventor (or inventors) and the U.S. government, providing the owner of the patent with the right to exclude others from making, using, selling, offering to sell, and importing the invention in the U.S. for a specific length of time in exchange for a complete description of how to make and use the invention.[4]

How Have These Forms of Intellectual Property Protection Evolved in the U.S.?

The laws surrounding copyrights, trademarks, trade secrets, and patents are constantly changing to adapt to and address problems which result from various advances in technology. For example, as the number of Internet users has increased, the concept of global commerce has changed. This new form of electronic commerce has created a new set of problems in intellectual property law. In particular, the laws with respect to copyrights and trademarks had to evolve from protecting traditional forms of media, such as print, to new forms of electronic media operating in a nontraditional medium called cyberspace.

A basic understanding of how intellectual property has evolved helps to appreciate the economic value and strategic importance of intellectual property. The United States Constitution provides protection for copyrights and patents in Article I, Section 8, Clause 8 where it states:

> The Congress shall have the power...to promote the progress of science and the useful arts by securing for limited times for the authors and inventors the exclusive right to their respective writings and discoveries.

In 1790, Congress passed the first copyright statute with general revisions occurring in 1831 and 1870. In 1909 major revisions to the copyright laws were adopted. In the 1950s, Congress began studies and conducted hearings lasting two decades that resulted in many of the copyright laws being rewritten. These laws were implemented on January 1, 1978. In 1989, Congress made additional changes to the copyright laws which allowed the U.S. to join the Berne Convention. The Berne Convention is a multilateral copyright treaty that gives a work the same level of protection in each member nation as that nation gives to works of its own citizens.

Like copyrights, patents have their Constitutional basis in Article I, Section 8, Clause 8. However, the role of patents in society goes back to the time of Aristotle (4th century B.C.). Aristotle referred to patents in his book "Politics," where he wrote about a reward system for inventors of useful things. In the late 15th century, the Venetian Senate passed an act that provided for the practice of granting patents. Surprisingly, many characteristics of today's patent statute are found in this Act. It was also during this time that the term "patent" had its origin. It comes from the Latin word "patere" which means "to be open." During the 16th century, the Italians introduced the idea of providing legal protection for inventions. In the 17th century, the British introduced the Statute of Monopolies which allowed for a review of all patents and eliminated all those that were not based on true inventions. Patents were introduced in the American colonies between 1640 and 1776 and were granted by the individual colonies. To maintain uniformity with respect to the granting of patents, the Constitutional Convention of 1789 came forth with Article I, Section 8, Clause 8. Congress passed the first U.S. patent statute in May 1790 and later revised the patent system in 1836. This revision changed the system from a registration system, where an application was submitted and a patent awarded, to the presentday examination system, where the application is reviewed. As greater demands were placed on the patent system, new rules evolved. Late in the 19th century, the patent structure began to evolve to its present form, rooted in the 1952 Patent Act.

During the 1960s and 1970s getting a patent upheld was difficult in many federal circuit courts because of the diverse interpretations of the patent law in the different circuits. To unify the interpretation of the patent laws, Congress passed the Federal Courts Improvement Act in 1982 that created the new Court of Appeals for the Federal Circuit (CAFC). A primary function of the CAFC is to hear all patent appeals from the federal district courts. The formation of the CAFC has increased the value of patents by making appellate review more predictable.

In 1994, the Uruguay Round Agreements Act (URAA) was enacted. The URAA implemented significant changes to the U.S. patent system, with several changes becoming effective on June 8, 1995 and the remaining changes implemented on January 1, 1996. The URAA resulted in the following key changes to the U.S. patent system:

(1) The term of a U.S. utility patent changed from 17 years from the issue date to 20 years from the filing date for all patents issuing from applications filed after June 8, 1995.

(2) The *provisional patent application* (further explained in Chapter Two) was introduced.

(3) Patent rights were extended to exclude others from *offering to sell* and *importing* the invention in the U.S.

Unlike copyrights and patents, Congress' power to regulate trademarks does not come from Article I, Section 8, Clause 8 of the U.S. Constitution. Instead, it is based on Article I, Section 8, Clause 3, which regulates commerce. The first modern federal trademark statute was enacted by Congress in 1905. The present trademark statute took effect in 1947 and is known as the Lanham Act.[5] In 1984, the Lanham Act was amended by Congress to prohibit counterfeiting and redefine the term "trademark" to clarify that trademarks may distinguish unique products and products whose source is unknown by name to customers. In 1989 the Trademark Law Revision Act took effect, making many changes to the Lanham Act and, in particular, allowing a trademark application to be filed based on *intent to use*. In 1996, the Federal Trademark Dilution Act took effect, providing protection for famous trademarks against uses that dilute the distinctiveness of the mark or tarnish or disparage it.

Trade secret law differs from copyright, trademark, and patent law in that until recently, it was largely based on state law, not federal law. In 1939, the criterion that influenced the development of trade secret law in most states was set forth in the 1939 Restatement of Torts. In 1979, the American Bar Association proposed the Uniform Trade Secrets Act and approximately 40 states adopted it with various modifications. In 1995, the Restatement of Torts was updated with the Restatement of Unfair Competition and, in 1996, the U.S.

enacted the Economic Espionage Act. This Act amends Title 18 of the United States Code such that it prevents trade secret theft by:

(1) a foreign entity; or

(2) anyone in general.

The definition of a trade secret in the Economic Espionage Act reflects Congress' attempt at trying to keep pace with the changes in technology. The common trend observed in the evolution of intellectual property protection is that technology, information accessibility, and global competition have caused changes in the law, moving from a localized focus to a global perspective.

More Information about Copyrights, Trademarks, Trade Secrets, and Patents

COPYRIGHTS

Copyrights protect "original works of authorship fixed in any tangible medium of expression."[6] Note that the work must be fixed in a tangible medium of expression. Thus, if the author has not notated or recorded the work, a copyright cannot protect it. Works of authorship include the following categories:

- literary works
- musical works
- dramatic works
- pantomimes and choreographic works
- pictorial, graphic, and sculptural works
- motion pictures and other audiovisual works

- sound recordings

- architectural works

These categories have very broad interpretations. For example, a computer software program qualifies as a literary work, whereas a globe or a map is considered as a pictorial, graphic, or sculptural work. Conversely, a design for a useful article or an article having a naturally useful function beyond simply portraying the appearance of the article is not protectable by a copyright. However, a copyright may protect the design if it incorporates pictorial, graphic, or sculptural features identified separately from and existing independently of the useful aspects of the article. For example, in *Donald Bruce & Co. v. B.N. Multi Com Corp.*[7] a ring was found copyrightable, because its sole utilitarian function is to portray the appearance of the article. Here, it did not matter whether the useful aspects of the ring were separable from its sculptural aspects. Contrasting this was *Magnussen Furniture, Inc. v. Collezione Europa USA, Inc.*,[8] where a table was found as not copyrightable because the utilitarian aspects of the table are inseparable from its sculptural features.

Many people have the misconception that if they simply write their idea down, a copyright automatically protects it. This is not true. A copyright will only protect how the idea is expressed, not the actual idea, which is protected by a trade secret or a patent. Also, copyrights do not protect short phrases such as slogans or unique names for products, these are protected as trademarks.

WARNING: Copyrights do not protect ideas, procedures, processes, systems, methods of operations, concepts, principles, or discoveries, regardless of the form in which it is described, explained, illustrated, or embodied in such work.[9]

The Copyright Act gives no definition for "an author." However, it is well understood that an author is the person who creates the copyrighted work; this is provided by the Constitution and several Supreme Court Decisions.[10,11,12] An exception to this definition occurs when the work is a result of a *work made for hire*. When this situation occurs, the employer, not the employee, is considered the author.[13]

A **work made for hire** results when:

(1) an employee prepares a work within the scope of his or her employment; or

(2) a work is specially ordered or commissioned for use as a contribution to a collective work, as a part of a motion picture or other audiovisual work, as a translation, as a supplementary work, as a compilation, as an instructional text, as a test, as answer material for a test, or as an atlas, if the parties expressly agree in a written instrument signed by them that the work shall be considered a work made for hire . . .[14]

Note that the second half of the work made for hire definition requires that a written agreement must be in place. Often, institutions of higher education will include a definition of work made for hire in their intellectual property policies.

TIP: If you are working in academia, review your institution's intellectual property policy to find out what qualifies as a work made for hire.

In sharp contrast to academia, employees of the U.S. government who create a copyrightable work on the job cannot claim a copyright in the work and neither can the U.S. government. "Copyright protection is not available for any work of the United States Government, . . ."[15]

Copyright protection is established from the moment the work is fixed in a tangible medium of expression, such as a written manuscript or a computer program. The work does not have to be published to qualify for copyright protection and copyright registration is voluntary. However, the copyright must be registered in order to sue for infringement in the U.S. Registering a copyright is an easy and inexpensive process involving:

(1) obtaining an application form from the U.S. Copyright Office (See Appendix I);

(2) completing the application; and

(3) submitting the completed application, along with a nonreturnable copy or copies of the work, and a nonrefundable filing fee ($20.00) to the U.S. Copyright Office.

The registration takes effect the day the Copyright Office receives all of the required elements. Usually, it takes about 5 to 6 months to receive the certificate of registration. A copyright certificate is shown in Fig. 1.1.

The copyright is identified by placing a notice on copies of the work. Typically the notice includes the symbol ©, or the word "copyright"; the year of first publication of the work; and the name of the owner of the copyright. The following is an example of a copyright notice:

© 1998 Joy L. Bryant

The notice informs the world of copyright ownership by identifying the copyright owner and showing the year of first publication.

CERTIFICATE OF REGISTRATION

This Certificate issued under the seal of the Copyright Office in accordance with title 17, United States Code, attests that registration has been made for the work identified below.The information on this certificate has been made a part of the Copyright Office records.

Marybeth Peters

REGISTER OF COPYRIGHTS
United States of America

OFFICIAL SEAL

FORM TX
For a Literary Work
UNITED STATES COPYRIGHT OFFICE

TX 4 – 595 – 820

EFFECTIVE DATE OF REGISTRATION

JUN 0 2 1997
Month   Day   Year

DO NOT WRITE ABOVE THIS LINE. IF YOU NEED MORE SPACE, USE A SEPARATE CONTINUATION SHEET.

TITLE OF THIS WORK ▼

A GUIDE TO PROTECTING AN IDEA

PREVIOUS OR ALTERNATIVE TITLES ▼

PUBLICATION AS A CONTRIBUTION If this work was published as a contribution to a periodical, serial, or collection, give information about the collective work in which the contribution appeared. **Title of Collective Work ▼**

If published in a periodical or serial give: **Volume ▼**   **Number ▼**   **Issue Date ▼**   **On Pages ▼**

NAME OF AUTHOR ▼

JOHN J. SMITH

DATES OF BIRTH AND DEATH
Year Born ▼   Year Died ▼
1963

Was this contribution to the work a "work made for hire"?
[ ] Yes
[X] No

AUTHOR'S NATIONALITY OR DOMICILE
Name of Country
OR { Citizen of ▶ United States
    { Domiciled in ▶

WAS THIS AUTHOR'S CONTRIBUTION TO THE WORK
Anonymous? [ ] Yes [X] No
Pseudonymous? [ ] Yes [X] No
If the answer to either of these questions is "Yes," see detailed instructions.

NATURE OF AUTHORSHIP Briefly describe nature of the material created by this author in which copyright is claimed. ▼

All text, including title, excluding cover artwork

NAME OF AUTHOR ▼

DATES OF BIRTH AND DEATH
Year Born ▼   Year Died ▼

Was this contribution to the work a "work made for hire"?
[ ] Yes
[ ] No

AUTHOR'S NATIONALITY OR DOMICILE
Name of Country
OR { Citizen of ▶
    { Domiciled in ▶

WAS THIS AUTHOR'S CONTRIBUTION TO THE WORK
Anonymous? [ ] Yes [ ] No
Pseudonymous? [ ] Yes [ ] No
If the answer to either of these questions is "Yes," see detailed instructions.

NATURE OF AUTHORSHIP Briefly describe nature of the material created by this author in which copyright is claimed. ▼

NAME OF AUTHOR ▼

DATES OF BIRTH AND DEATH
Year Born ▼   Year Died ▼

Was this contribution to the work a "work made for hire"?
[ ] Yes
[ ] No

AUTHOR'S NATIONALITY OR DOMICILE
Name of Country
OR { Citizen of ▶
    { Domiciled in ▶

WAS THIS AUTHOR'S CONTRIBUTION TO THE WORK
Anonymous? [ ] Yes [ ] No
Pseudonymous? [ ] Yes [ ] No
If the answer to either of these questions is "Yes," see detailed instructions.

NATURE OF AUTHORSHIP Briefly describe nature of the material created by this author in which copyright is claimed. ▼

YEAR IN WHICH CREATION OF THIS WORK WAS COMPLETED This information must be given in all cases.
1997 ◀ Year

DATE AND NATION OF FIRST PUBLICATION OF THIS PARTICULAR WORK Complete this information ONLY if this work has been published.
Month ▶ May   Day ▶ 29   Year ▶ 1997
United States ◀ Nation

COPYRIGHT CLAIMANT(S) Name and address must be given even if the claimant is the same as the author given in space 2.▼

JOHN J SMITH
123 ANYWHERE ST
ANYTOWN, USA 98765

APPLICATION RECEIVED
JUN 0 2 1997
ONE DEPOSIT RECEIVED
TWO DEPOSITS RECEIVED
JUN 0 2 1997
REMITTANCE NUMBER AND DATE

TRANSFER If the claimant(s) named here in space 4 are different from the author(s) named in space 2, give a brief statement of how the claimant(s) obtained ownership of the copyright.▼

MORE ON BACK ▶ • Complete all applicable spaces (numbers 5-11) on the reverse side of this page.
• See detailed instructions.   • Sign the form at line 10.

DO NOT WRITE HERE

Page 1 of ____ pages

FIGURE 1.1

A copyright certificate. The certificate of registration is attached directly to the originally filed application. Each registration is assigned a number and an effective date of registration.

This notice is no longer required for copyright protection. However, including it will prevent a defendant from claiming "innocent infringement," i.e., he or she did not realize that the work is protected.

> **Copyright infringement** is the unauthorized use, importation of copies, or violation of the exclusive rights provided by a copyright.[16]

Copyright infringement occurs when the accused work is essentially the same as the copyrighted work and the accused work is copied from the copyrighted work. Lawsuits resulting from copyright infringement are litigated in Federal District Court. The remedies for infringement include:

(1) an injunction or order to stop;

(2) impounding and disposition of infringing articles;

(3) damages and profits; and

(4) possibly court costs and attorney's fees.

Copyright infringement may be unknowing, or it may be deliberate or willful. If willful copyright infringement occurs, it is a federal offense and is punishable by a maximum penalty of 1 year in prison and/or a maximum fine of $250,000. One example of willful or deliberate copyright infringement that is currently taking place is on the Internet. Many people are putting up websites that contain articles and/or are subscribing to bulletin board services where individuals can post information. These activities have resulted in some individuals being found guilty of posting copyrighted articles without obtaining permission from the author. Such was the case in *Religious Technology Center v. Lerma.*[17] The judge found that a former Scientology Church member who posted many pages of copyrighted Church documents to the Internet had infringed one or more copyrights. This type of infringement was deliberate.

> *TIP:* If you are planning to post a copyrighted article on the Internet, be sure to get permission from the author or owner of the copyright (author and/or publisher).

A sale of an infringing work does not have to occur to be considered copyright infringement. The court had found in *Psihoyos v. Liberation, Inc.*[18] that distributing a single complimentary copy of an infringing image to a member of the public is copyright infringement.

If someone has a copyright in one particular medium, the copyright extends to other media. Such was the case in *Castle Rock Entertainment v. Carol Publishing Group.*[19] In this case, a trivia quiz book was published based on the events that took place in the television show "Seinfeld." According to the judge, these events are not mere facts that others can exploit; they are creative expressions within a derivative work. Thus, using this information without permission was not *fair use,* and Carol Publishing Group was found to have infringed on the copyright of the television show, "Seinfeld."

Fair use is a defense to copyright infringement. It is defined in 17 U.S.C. §107 as "the fair use of a copyrighted work, including such use by reproduction in copies or phono records or by any other means specified by section 106 and 106A, for purposes such as criticism, comment, news reporting, teaching (including multiple copies for classroom use), scholarship, or research."

Four factors are considered when determining whether the use of a work is fair use:[20]

(1) the purpose and character of the use, including whether such use is of a commercial nature or is for nonprofit educational purposes;

(2) the nature of the copyrighted work;

(3) the amount and substantiality of the portion used in relation to the copyrighted work as whole; and

(4) the effect of the use upon the potential market for or value of the copyrighted work.

These four factors are applied on a case-by-case basis to determine whether fair use applies.

> *TIP:* When in doubt about potential copyright infringement, ask for the author or owner's permission.

Asking for copyright permission is easy. Write a letter to the owner of the copyrighted material. Notify the owner of the precise material to be used by identifying the publication, page number, and lines or figures. Let the owner know where the material will be used, such as a book having a certain title, etc., and that an acknowledgment of the work will be provided.

A copyright is enforceable for the life of the author plus 50 years. In the instances where more than one author has created a work, the copyright term extends to 50 years after the last surviving author's death. If the copyrighted work results from some type of employment agreement or work for hire, the copyright protection is limited to 75 years from the date of publication or 100 years from the date of creation, whichever is shorter. Anonymous works remain protected for the same amount of time as works for hire. As of January 1, 1978, copyright renewal is no longer required.

TRADEMARKS

Trademarks serve a useful purpose in the commercial sector where they identify and distinguish the source of goods or services of one party from those of others. Trademarks apply to:

- words
- slogans
- designs
- colors
- sounds
- pictures or other symbols

that are used to identify and distinguish goods. Some familiar examples of trademarks include: the golden arches symbol for McDonald's; the slogan "Intel Inside" for Intel's computer chips; the pink color for Owens–Corning fiberglass; and the NBC chimes. Unlike copyrights, trademarks are tied to products and give consumers a certain level of expectation when they purchase a particular trademarked product. Trademarks function in four ways:

(1) they identify one person's goods from goods sold by someone else;

(2) they signify that all of the trademarked goods come from only one source;

(3) they show that all of the trademarked goods are of an equal quality; and

(4) they are used to help promote, advertise, and sell goods.

There are various marks besides trademarks. These marks include trade names, service marks, collective marks, and certification marks.

A **trade name** is any name used to identify one's business or vocation.

A **service mark** identifies and distinguishes the services of one person from the services of others. For example, titles, character names, and other distinctive features of radio or television programs may be registered as service marks.

A **collective mark** is a trademark or a service mark that is used by members of a cooperative, an association, or other collective group or organization.

A **certification mark** is any word, name, symbol, or device, or any combination thereof, used by a person other than its owner to certify regional or other origin, material, mode of manufacture, quality, accuracy, or other characteristics of that person's good or services. In addition, the certification mark may be used to identify that members of a union or other organization performed the work or labor on the goods or services.

Trademarks should be used along with a generic term or descriptive word to emphasize the "brand" aspect of the mark. This keeps the mark from losing its distinctiveness. Some marks, such as aspirin and escalator, have become generic because the courts found that consumers thought that the name was a generic name for a particular type of product.

> *TIP:* To prevent a trademark from becoming generic, use the mark as an adjective.

Trademarks do not have to be registered to be used. However, if a trademark is registered, it may be registered in a particular state, federally, or both. State registered trademarks are afforded protection by state common law. Federally registered marks are protected under the Lanham Act and carry the symbol ® next to them. Marks that are registered both on the state and the federal level are given the benefit of state law being able to expand the rights of the federal registration. This is accomplished by the states granting more rights to prevent consumer confusion[21] and making it easier to meet the requirements needed to prove that infringement has occurred.[22]

> *TIP:* To reserve rights in an unregistered mark, simply put the designator ™ (for trademark) or ℠ (for service mark) next to the mark. It is not necessary to have a trademark registration or even a pending application for the mark to use these designators.

> *TIP:* Registering a trademark in a particular state is usually less expensive than federally registering the mark. To obtain a state registration, consult an intellectual property attorney in the state where you want protection.

Applying for a trademark is fairly easy and may or may not require the assistance of an intellectual property attorney. To apply for a federal trademark:

(1) Obtain the trademark application forms from the U.S. Patent and Trademark Office (U.S.P.T.O.) (see Appendix I).

(2) Decide whether to apply based on a "use" application, or an "intent-to-use" application. "Use" means that the mark is already being used in interstate commerce or in commerce between the U.S. and another country. "Intent-to-use" applies when there is a bona fide intention to use the mark in interstate commerce or between the U.S. and another country.

(3) Properly complete the application and submit it to the U.S.P.T.O.

> *WARNING:* A U.S. registration only protects the mark in the U.S. and its territories. To protect the mark outside the U.S., one must file in each country under its laws.

Once the U.S.P.T.O. receives the application, an Examining Attorney reviews the application to make sure it meets all of the requirements and that the mark is registerable. In particular, the mark must be distinctive, meaning that there is no cause for confusion between the applicant's mark and a registered mark. The mark cannot be:

(1) merely descriptive in relation to the applicant's goods or services;

(2) a feature of the goods or services;

(3) a geographic term; or

(4) a surname.

If the mark is registerable, it is approved for publication in the U.S.P.T.O.'s Official Gazette, a weekly publication of the U.S.P.T.O. This publication starts a 30-day opposition period where any party believing it may be damaged by the registration of the mark may file an *opposition* to registration. The opposition proceeding takes place between the applicant and the opposing party and is an administrative proceeding before the Trademark Trial and Appeal Board. If no one opposes the registration of the mark or if the opposition is unsuccessful, the U.S.P.T.O. issues a registration certificate. This process, without opposition, takes approximately 1 year to complete.

Trademark infringement occurs when a person:

(1) uses in commerce any reproduction, counterfeit, copy, or colorable imitation of a registered mark in connection with the sale, offering for sale, distribution, or advertising of any goods or services on or in connection with which such use is likely to cause confusion, mistake or deceive the public; or

(2) reproduces, counterfeits, copies, or colorably imitates a registered mark and applies the reproduction, counterfeit, copy or colorable imitation to labels, signs, prints, packages, wrappers, receptacles, or advertisements intended to be used in commerce in connection with the sale, offering for sale, distribution, or advertising of goods or services on or in connection with which such use is likely to cause confusion, or to cause mistake, or to deceive.[23]

In addition, uses that dilute, tarnish, or disparage the distinctiveness of a famous mark are also infringement under the Federal Trademark Dilution Act.[24]

One example of trademark confusion is the case of *Meridian Mutual Insurance Company v. Meridian Insurance Group, Inc.*[25] Not only was Meridian Mutual Insurance Company receiving checks made out to Meridian Insurance Group, Inc. but customers were being misdirected by Meridian Insurance Group, Inc.'s 800 number. The court granted a preliminary injunction against Meridian Insurance Group, Inc. to end the confusion.

As with copyright infringement, trademark infringement has become a problem on the Internet. Many companies are discovering that their trademarks have been registered by others as domain names. In *Hasbro, Inc. v. Internet Entertainment Group*,[26] Hasbro, Inc. obtained a federal court order to block Internet Entertainment Group from using the name "candyland.com" for an adults-only Internet site. Internet Entertainment Group's use of Hasbro, Inc.'s trademark serves as an example of a famous mark being tarnished. In *Panavision International L.P. v. Toeppen*,[27] the court found that an Internet user violated the Federal Trademark Dilution Act by registering the domain name "panavision.com" with the intention of selling it back to Panavision International. The misuse of trademarks on the Internet has resulted in an increase in the number of trademark-related lawsuits being filed.

Trademark rights can last indefinitely, provided the owner continues to use the mark and properly renews the registration.[28] Federal trademark registrations have a term of 10 years and are renewable in 10-year increments. However, between the 5th and 6th year after the initial registration date, the owner must file an affidavit showing current use of the mark to keep the registration from being canceled.

TRADE SECRETS

Trade secret protection applies to confidential business information, such as new ways of conducting business and not yet patented inventions. Examples of information protectable by trade secrets include all forms and types of:

- financial, business, scientific, technical, economic or engineering information
- patterns
- plans
- compilations
- program devices

- formulas
- designs
- prototypes
- methods, techniques, processes, procedures
- software programs or codes

Trade secret protection requires responsibility. To maintain a trade secret, the owner must do everything possible to keep the information secret. This responsibility is not limited to the owner but also extends to the employees of a company. To prove that the information is confidential, the employees must actually treat it as a secret. This is done by marking information as confidential, having training programs, and having employees report suspicious activities.

TIP: If you are in the corporate environment and are protecting information as a trade secret, be sure that others within the company are aware that the information is proprietary and that they have a duty to treat the information as secret.

Not only must the information be kept as secret, but it must also have independent economic value that results from the information not being generally known to or available to the public. An example of a well-kept trade secret is the formula for the Coca-Cola® soft drink, which clearly has an independent economic value.

The cost of trade secret protection is equivalent to the costs associated with keeping the information a secret. No registration or application process is involved. Instead, the owner must keep the information confidential. A confidentiality agreement should be used if the proprietary information must be revealed to a third party. Failure to keep the information confidential or revealing the information to an outside interest without a confidentiality agreement will make it difficult to enforce the trade secret protection. However, if a third party obtains the trade secret information through illegal activity, the price for violating the trade secret can be high.

The Economic Espionage Act makes it a federal offense to steal trade secrets. Fines can be as much at $5,000,000 and imprisonment up to 10 years for domestic theft of trade secrets. In addition, the Economic Espionage Act extends to activities outside the U.S. if the offender is a U.S. citizen or an organization organized under U.S. or state laws. The FBI handles the investigation and U.S. Attorneys may prosecute the alleged offenders. In addition, these cases are to be resolved quicker than civil suits that take place in the state court system. However, the Economic Espionage Act has its drawbacks. In particular, one cannot be charged for revealing a trade secret if there is no intent to economically gain from it.

The potential for disclosure of a trade secret occurs when an employee leaves a company for a competitor. Such was the case for Dow Chemical Company[29] who accused General Electric of hiring former Dow engineers and sales executives and placing them in similar jobs. Dow alleged that such placement would cause the former employees to reveal Dow's trade secrets. They eventually settled the suit out of court.

In *Injection Research Specialists v. Polaris Indus.*[30] a jury awarded $57 million to Injection Research Specialists. Apparently, Injection Research Specialists had shown Polaris a prototype for a fuel injection system under a confidentiality agreement. After several months of negotiations, Polaris claimed to be no longer interested. Several years later, Polaris produced a fuel injected snowmobile. Injection Research Specialists claimed that Polaris sent the ideas to its partner, Fuji Heavy industries, violating the confidentiality agreement. Polaris claimed that they developed the engine independently. The jury disagreed and ordered Polaris to pay $34 million and Fuji to pay $23 million to Injection Research Specialists.

The length of trade secret protection is indefinite, meaning that the protection is good until one reveals the secret to a third party, outside a confidentiality agreement, or someone independently discovers it. This risk must be considered when opting for trade secret protection. However, for companies like Coca-Cola, trade secret protection has far outlasted patent protection.

PATENTS

Patents protect structures or methods that apply technological concepts. More specifically, patents protect:

- Machines
- Articles of manufacture
- Methods or processes
- Compositions of matter
- Improvements to machines, articles of manufacture, methods or processes, or compositions of matter
- Plants
- Ornamental Designs

A patent is both a legal document and a technical document. It is comparable to a contract between the inventor and the government where the inventor agrees to:

(1) describe how to make and use the invention; and

(2) disclose the best mode known to the inventor at the time to carry out the invention.

In exchange for this description and teaching of the invention, the government provides the inventor with *the right to prevent others* from making, using, selling, offering for sale, or importing the invention in the U.S. Many people think that if an invention is patented, the owner now has the right to make, use, sell, offer sale, or import the invention in the U.S. This is not necessarily true. A patent gives the owner the right to prevent others from making, using, selling, offering for sale, or importing the invention in the U.S. Simply because a person has received a patent for an invention, does not necessarily mean that he or she may make, use, sell, offer for sale, or import the invention in the U.S. if doing so violates any law or someone else's rights. For example, if a person obtains a patent for a new drug, the drug is subject to FDA approval before it may be made, used, sold, offered for sale, or imported in the U.S. Lastly, a person may not make, use, sell, offer for sale, or import into the U.S. his or her own patented invention if it infringes on someone else's patent without getting permission from that person. Suppose a person has received a patent for an engine. The engine uses a patented piston that is not commercially available. The owner of the patented engine would have to get permission from the owner of the patented piston to produce the engine.

> *WARNING:* An issued patent does not serve as a market clearance for the product. Having a patent does not necessarily allow the inventor to make, use, sell, offer for sale, or import the patented invention in the U.S. if the invention infringes on someone else's patent.

Every patent has claims that define the invention. The claims precisely define the inventor's exclusive right in the technology. The claims are similar to a real estate deed that explains the exact dimensions of a piece of property.

The **claims** are the part of the patent that set forth the definition of the technology that is exclusively owned by the patentee for the term of the patent.

Each claim has parts or elements that define the invention. When patent infringement occurs, the alleged infringing device is compared with the claims in the patent. *Literal infringement* occurs when each and every element found in the claims is also found in the infringing device. However, one should note that if additional elements are included in the infringing device that are not included in the claims, the device may still be literally infringing on the patent. For example, literal infringement was found[31] when one company patented A+B+C and a second company patented A+B+C+D. The second company literally infringed the claims in the first company's patent. If literal infringement cannot be found, then infringement may be found under the *Doctrine of Equivalents*. The Doctrine of Equivalents allows the literal language of a claim to be interpreted in such a way that if the accused device performs substantially the same function in substantially the same way to obtain substantially the same result as the claimed invention, the device is infringing. If someone is found liable for patent infringement, the standard remedy is an injunction and damages. The damages are usually measured based on a reasonable royalty or lost profits. These damages can be in the hundreds of millions of dollars. For example, Haworth, Inc.[32] was awarded damages of $207.6 million for Steelcase, Inc.'s infringement of two patents for electrified office wall panels. In addition, Haworth, Inc. also received a third award of $3.8 million for Steelcase, Inc.'s infringement involving a third patent for articulating keyboard shelves. Clearly, patent protection has grown to be a valuable asset.

Filing a patent application is not as easy as filing for a copyright or trademark. Unlike copyrights and trademarks, there is no form. Instead, a patent application is more like a Last Will and Testament. Like a Will, every patent application must contain certain sections and the way each section is completed is specific to the invention itself. The patent application is filed in the U.S. Patent and Trademark Office (U.S.P.T.O.) where it undergoes examination by a Patent Examiner. The Examiner conducts a search of the literature (mostly patent) and reviews the application to see if the invention is new, useful, and not obvious. Usually, the Examiner rejects the application, shifting the burden to prove patentability of the invention to the applicant, who must present arguments to overcome the Examiner's rejections. The application is allowed if the applicant is successful in showing that the invention is new, useful, and not obvious. Upon receiving an indication of a notice of allowance, an issue fee must be paid, and then the patent issues. Figure 1.2 provides an example of a utility patent.

There are three types of patents: utility, design and plant. Utility patents are the most common type of patent. The U.S.P.T.O. issues utility patents for those inventions which function in a unique way to produce a useful result. As of June 8, 1995, a utility patent is enforceable for 20 years from the filing date of the patent application. Utility patents which were in force on, or issued for applications filed before June 8, 1995 have a term of 17 years from the issue date or 20 years from the filing date, whichever is longer. Design patents are reserved for the unique ornamental or visible shape of an object. A design patent will not protect the functional aspects of an invention. For example, a design patent may protect the look of a vase but not the vase itself. Design patents are enforceable for 14 years from the date of issue. Lastly, plant patents provide protection for asexually reproduced plants such as a peach tree. However, plant patents do not protect tuber propagated plants or plants found in an uncultivated state. These and sexually reproduced plants are protected in other ways (discussed in Chapter Two). Plant patents are enforceable for 17 years

US005701709A

United States Patent [19]

Dixon, III

[11] **Patent Number:** 5,701,709

[45] **Date of Patent:** Dec. 30, 1997

[54] **INSULATION SUPPORT SYSTEM FOR METAL FRAME CONSTRUCTION AND METHOD RELATING THERETO**

[76] Inventor: **John R. Dixon, III**, 2509 General Forrest Cir., Virginia Beach, Va. 23454

[21] Appl. No.: **757,302**

[22] Filed: **Nov. 27, 1996**

[51] Int. Cl.⁶ E04B 1/74

[52] U.S. Cl. 52/404.1; 52/742.13; 52/742.1; 52/474; 52/508

[58] Field of Search 52/742.13, 742.1, 52/404.1, 404.3, 407.3, 482, 483.1, 508, 356, 474

[56] **References Cited**

U.S. PATENT DOCUMENTS

943,696	12/1909	Mooney et al.	52/356
969,213	9/1910	Gold et al.	52/356 X
1,504,325	8/1924	Collins	52/356
1,685,247	9/1928	Selway	52/356
1,814,202	7/1931	Winget	52/356
2,076,728	4/1937	Keller	52/482 X
2,989,790	6/1961	Brown	52/742.13
3,363,371	1/1968	Villalobos	52/356 X
3,850,073	11/1974	Hayes .	
4,177,618	12/1979	Felter	52/742.13
4,385,477	5/1983	Walls et al.	52/404.3 X
4,523,531	6/1985	Bishara .	
4,594,828	6/1986	Taylor .	
4,712,347	12/1987	Sperber	52/742.13 X
4,844,651	7/1989	Partridge .	
5,230,597	7/1993	Nuttall .	

5,287,674	2/1994	Sperber	52/742.13
5,365,716	11/1994	Munson	52/742.13
5,412,919	5/1995	Pellock .	
5,561,957	10/1996	Gauthier .	

Primary Examiner—Robert Canfield

Attorney, Agent, or Firm—Joy L. Bryant

[57] **ABSTRACT**

An insulation support system for metal frame construction is provided. The system comprises an insulation support material and a metal frame. The metal frame comprises a plurality of metal members, wherein at least two opposing metal members have at least one portion thereof stamped out to protrude on one side. An exterior sheathing is attached to an opposing side of the metal frame. The stamped out protrusion engages the insulation support material. This system is particularly useful for steel frame construction and does not require the use of adhesives or additional tools. The method of the present invention involves providing a metal frame having a plurality of metal members wherein at least two opposing members have at least one portion thereof stamped out to protrude on one side and an exterior sheathing attached to an opposing side. An insulation support material is engaged and tensioned on the stamped out protruded portions of the opposing metal members forming a cavity between the insulation support material and the exterior sheathing. Insulation is blown into the cavity. This method allows for positive restraint of the insulation support material and high density insulation. Thus, a high "R" value is achieved. In addition, installation is independent of weather conditions, requires no additional tools, and is more efficient than those systems currently used.

18 Claims, 4 Drawing Sheets

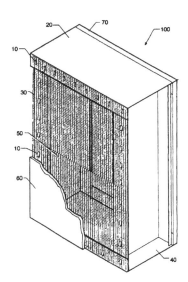

FIGURE 1.2 *(continues)*

An example of a utility patent. Note the amount of written detail that is used to describe the invention. This description instructs a person how

U.S. Patent   Dec. 30, 1997   Sheet 1 of 4   **5,701,709**

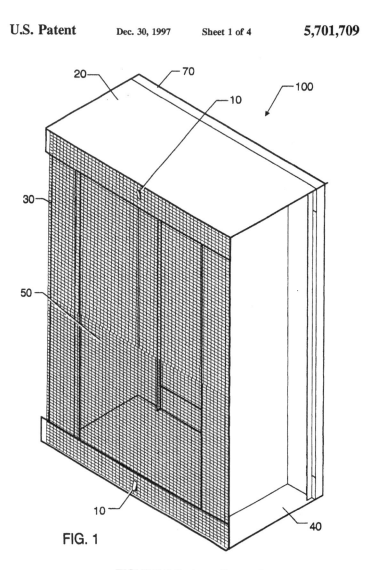

FIG. 1

FIGURE 1.2 *(continues)*

to make and use the invention. Also note that several views of drawings are required to depict the invention.

U.S. Patent   Dec. 30, 1997   Sheet 2 of 4   **5,701,709**

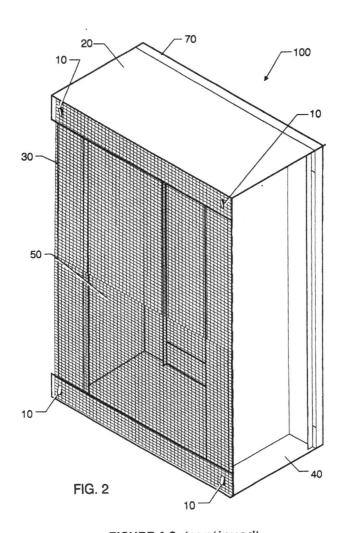

FIG. 2

FIGURE 1.2 *(continued)*

U.S. Patent   Dec. 30, 1997   Sheet 3 of 4   **5,701,709**

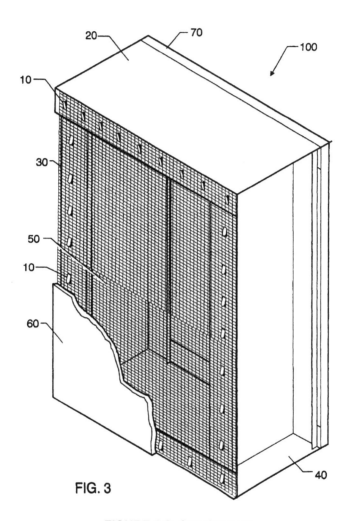

FIG. 3

FIGURE 1.2 *(continues)*

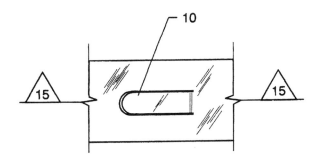

FIG. 4A

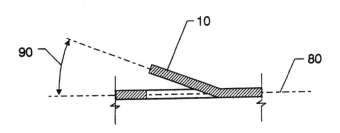

FIG. 4B

FIGURE 1.2 *(continued)*

5,701,709

1

INSULATION SUPPORT SYSTEM FOR METAL FRAME CONSTRUCTION AND METHOD RELATING THERETO

BACKGROUND OF THE INVENTION

The present invention relates to insulation support systems. In particular, it relates to blown-in insulation support systems for metal frame construction.

The blown in blanket (BIB) insulation system has demonstrated a higher thermal resistance per unit of thickness. In addition, the BIB insulation system also dramatically reduces the need for secondary caulking and sealants to reduce air infiltration, making it more desirable than fiberglass blanket (BATT) insulation. The BIB insulation system is comprised of standard chopped fiberglass or Rockwool insulation blown in place with a water and glue mist.

When installing BIB insulation in a wood frame building, a nylon netting or support material is first stapled to the wood frame. The BIB insulation is blown between the structural members and held in place by the nylon netting until the interior wall system is installed. The net tension plays an important role in determining the success of the BIB insulation. Insufficient tension on the net results in a low density insulation, a low "R" value, and thus a poor installation. For wood frame construction this is not a problem since the net is stapled in place.

However, when the BIB insulation was applied to metal frame structures, various problems were encountered. The nylon netting or support material could not be stapled to the metal frame. In turn, the netting was attached by adhering the net to the metal frame. In this process, the adhesive was first placed on the studs and allowed to dry to a predetermined degree of tackiness. The net was then applied to the tacky studs and pulled tight. It was at this point in the application process that problems were encountered. First, it was found that too much tension on the net resulted in the net being pulled off of the studs. When the net was installed using lower tension, a poor installation resulted. In addition, it was found that the adhesive was adversely affected by changes in the temperature and humidity. In cold and or high humidity conditions, the adhesive could not hold the netting at a tension which would retain the BIB insulation before the interior wall system was constructed. In addition, the adhesive took considerable time to apply and to dry.

One approach towards solving these problems was attaching the nylon netting to the metal framework using screws. However, this process was found to be expensive and time consuming. For the foregoing reasons, there is a need for a blown-in insulation support system for metal frame construction which is easy to use, time-saving and low in installation cost.

BRIEF SUMMARY OF THE INVENTION

An object of the present invention is to provide a blown-in insulation support system for metal frame construction.

Another object is to provide a blown-in insulation support system for metal frame construction which does not require the use of an adhesive.

Another object is to provide a blown-in insulation support system for metal construction which allows for construction independent of temperature and humidity conditions.

Another object is to provide a blown-in insulation support system which provides a mechanical means for support which is a part of the metal frame.

By the present invention, a blown-in insulation support system for metal frame construction is provided. The blown-

2

in insulation support system comprises an insulation support material and a metal frame comprising a plurality of metal members, wherein at least two opposing metal members have at least one portion thereof stamped out to protrude on one side and an exterior sheathing attached to an opposing side, and wherein the stamped out protrusion engages the insulation support material.

The insulation support material may be either nylon netting, fabric, reinforced material, or a thin, translucent cloth material. Most preferably, the insulation support material is nylon netting.

The metal members are either primary metal members or secondary metal members or a combination thereof and preferably are formed from steel. Each metal member has a longitudinal axis and the stamped portion and the longitudinal axis form an angle of protrusion.

In particular, a blown-in insulation support system for steel frame construction comprises a nylon net; and a steel frame comprising spaced apart steel top and bottom tracks and a plurality of parallel elongate steel studs extending between the top track and the bottom track spaced at intervals along the length of the track, wherein the top track, the bottom track and the elongate studs each have a longitudinal axis and each has at least one portion thereof stamped out to protrude on one side at an angle of about 20 degrees between the protruded portion and the longitudinal axis and an exterior sheathing attached to an opposing side; and wherein the stamped out protrusion engages the nylon net.

The method of the present invention involves providing a metal frame having a plurality of metal members wherein at least two opposing metal members have at least one portion thereof stamped out to protrude on one side and an exterior sheathing attached to an opposing side; engaging and tensioning an insulation support material on the stamped out protruded portions of the metal frame forming a cavity between the exterior sheathing and the insulation support material; and blowing insulation into the cavity.

The insulation support system for metal frame construction of the present invention allows for construction independent of temperature and humidity conditions. It also provides maximum tension of the insulation support material. Since no tools and adhesives are required, the number of steps in the construction process are greatly reduced.

BRIEF DESCRIPTION OF THE SEVERAL VIEWS OF THE DRAWING

FIG. 1 is an orthographic view of a typical wall showing an embodiment of the present invention.

FIG. 2 is an orthographic view of a typical wall showing a second embodiment of the present invention.

FIG. 3 is an orthographic view of a typical wall showing the preferred embodiment of the present invention.

FIG. 4A is a front view of the stamped out protruded portion of the present invention.

FIG. 4B is a cross-section view of the stamped out protruded portion of the present invention.

DETAILED DESCRIPTION OF THE INVENTION

Referring to the drawings, FIG. 1 is an orthographic view of a typical wall showing the insulation support system for metal frame construction of the present invention 100. In the figure, the primary metal member is a stud 30 and the secondary metal members are the metal top track 20 and the

FIGURE 1.2 *(continues)*

5,701,709

| 3 | 4 |

metal bottom track 40. In the figure, only the top and bottom tracks are shown to have at least one portion thereof stamped out to protrude on one side 10. The stamped out protrusion 10 is used to engage the insulation support material 50.

It is not necessary that all the metal members be stamped out nor is it necessary to stamp all sides of the metal members, but rather only the side which will be engaging the insulation support material needs to be stamped. Stamped is defined as forming a perforation in the metal such that one portion of the metal extends outward from the longitudinal axis of the metal member. This may be achieved by either using a hand held die punch or using traditional metal stamping techniques. The direction of the stamped out protrusion may be either upward, downward, right facing or left facing. The only requirement for the present invention is that at least one set of opposing metal members must be stamped to allow for engaging and tensioning the insulation support material. Opposing is defined as members across from one another. For example, the metal top track and the metal bottom track are stamped with the parallel elongated studs not being stamped or the parallel elongated studs are stamped with the metal top and bottom tracks not being stamped. At least one protrusion is needed per opposing metal member to engage the insulation support material. FIG. 1 shows two opposing metal members, the top track 20 and the bottom track 40, each having only one portion thereof stamped out to protrude 10 on the same side as sufficient to hold the insulation support material in place.

As an alternative embodiment of the invention, two opposing metal members, such as the top track and the bottom track, were stamped at each corner to protrude on the same side as shown in FIG. 2. In this embodiment, the two opposing metal members, the top track 20 and the bottom track 40, were stamped out to protrude 10 at opposing corners. The metal studs 30 were not stamped. The insulation support material 50 was engaged and tensioned on each protrusion 10.

FIG. 3 shows the most preferred embodiment where both the primary 30 and the secondary 20, 40 metal members have many stamped protrusions. In this case, the metal top track 20, the metal bottom track 40, and the metal studs 30 were all stamped more than one time to yield multiple protrusions. The insulation support material 50 was engaged with each stamped out protrusion providing optimum tension.

The drawings all depict a metal frame comprised of metal members having a standard track and stud configuration. However, as alternative embodiments the primary metal member could also be a joist where the secondary metal members may be either: a purlin or a channel of any configuration known to those skilled in the art. In addition, any combination of primary and secondary metal members may be used. However, a preferred embodiment is a track and stud configuration.

The metal members may be formed from any metal known to those skilled in the art such as steel, anodized aluminum, or sheet metal. Most preferably, the metal is steel.

The metal frame shown in FIG. 3 comprises spaced apart top 20 and bottom 40 tracks. A plurality of parallel elongate studs 30 extend between the top track 20 and the bottom track 40 and are spaced at intervals along the length of the track. The top track 20, bottom track 40, and elongate studs 30 each have a longitudinal axis and each has at least one portion thereof stamped out to protrude on one side forming an angle between the protruded portion 10 and the longitudinal axis. An angle of about 20 degrees is preferred. The

stamped out protrusion engages the insulation support material 50. The insulation support material 50, metal members 20, 30, and 40, and exterior sheathing 70 form a cavity in the wall where insulation is blown therebetween.

FIG. 4A is a front view of the stamped out protrusion 10 and FIG. 4B is a cross-sectional view of the stamped out protrusion 10 taken along line 15. The metal member has a longitudinal axis 80 and a stamped portion 10 such that an angle 90 is formed between the longitudinal axis 80 and stamped portion 10. The angle formed must be sufficient to hold the insulation support material without causing the support material to fall off the metal member. Any angle would satisfy this requirement. If the angle is 90 degrees, a means for preventing the insulation support material from sliding off of the protrusion may be employed. Such a means may be a barb, an arrowhead or simply an additional bend in the protrusion. The best results were found when an acute angle was formed between the stamped portion and the longitudinal axis. Most preferably an angle of about 20 degrees was found to be suitable for this application.

Although the protrusions of the present invention are stamped out of the metal member, as an alternative, a second member could be fastened onto the metal member to form a protrusion having the configuration mentioned above. For example a prestamped metal strip could be attached to the metal member using an adhesive, welding, or any other method of attachment known to those skilled in the art. However, the present invention preferably addresses a unibody construction wherein the protrusion is formed directly from the metal member.

Any insulation support material known to those skilled in the art may be used for the system of the present invention. However preferred types of insulation support material include: nylon netting, fabric, reinforced material, or a thin translucent cloth material known as Isomesh® commercially available from Ark-Seal Corporation. The stamped out protrusion engages the insulation support material by such methods as hooking onto the insulation support material or by piercing the material. Most preferably, the insulation support material is hooked on to the stamped out protrusions.

The method of the present invention involves providing a metal frame having a plurality of metal members wherein at least two opposing metal members have at least one portion thereof stamped out to protrude on one side and an exterior sheathing attached to an opposing side. An insulation support material is engaged and tensioned on the stamped out protruded portions of the metal frame such that a cavity forms between the exterior sheathing and the insulation support material. Lastly, insulation is blown into the cavity.

The system and method of the present invention allows for positive restraint of the insulation support material and high density insulation. Thus, a high "R" value is achieved. In addition, installation is independent of weather conditions, requires no additional tools and is more efficient than those systems currently used.

The following example illustrates the method of the present invention. This example is merely illustrative and intended to enable those skilled in the art to practice the invention in all of the embodiments flowing therefrom, and does not in any way limit the scope of the invention as defined in the claims.

EXAMPLE

Two steel tracks and two steel studs were stamped out using a hand held die punch to yield a protrusion having a

FIGURE 1.2 *(continued)*

5,701,709

5

20 degree angle between the protruded steel portion and the longitudinal axis of the steel track or stud. The tracks were die punched at 1.5 inch intervals along one edge where the studs were die punched at 2 inch intervals along one edge. The punched tracks and studs were assembled to form a frame following conventional construction fabrication techniques. The exterior sheathing was attached to the non-punched side of the top and bottom tracks. The nylon insulation support netting was first attached to the protrusions on the top track by hooking the netting over the protrusions. The netting was then extended downward, maintaining a slight tension, and hooked on to the protrusions on the bottom track. Lastly, the netting was secured to the studs by the installer running a hand over the protrusions in the direction of orientation. The orientation for the protrusions on the studs may be either upward, downward, left facing or right facing. Thus, a cavity was formed between the netting and the exterior sheathing. Lastly, a small opening was cut in the netting and the insulation was blown into the cavity using standard techniques.

What is claimed is:

1. A blown-in insulation support system for metal frame construction comprising:
   an insulation support material selected from the group consisting of: a nylon netting; a fabric; a reinforced material; and a thin translucent cloth material for holding insulation; and
   a metal frame comprising a plurality of metal members, wherein at least two opposing metal members have at least one portion thereof stamped out to protrude on one side and an exterior sheathing attached to an opposing side, and wherein each stamped out protrusion engages and tensions the insulation support material.

2. A blown-in insulation support system for metal frame construction according to claim 1, wherein the insulation support material is a nylon netting.

3. A blown-in insulation support system for metal frame construction according to claim 1, wherein the metal member is selected from the group consisting of: a primary metal member and a secondary metal member.

4. A blown-in insulation support system for metal frame construction according to claim 3, wherein the primary metal member is selected from the group consisting of: a stud and a joist; and the secondary metal member is selected from the group consisting of: a purlin; a channel; and a track.

5. A blown-in insulation support system for metal frame construction according to claim 1, wherein each metal member is formed from steel.

6. A blown-in insulation support system for metal frame construction according to claim 1, wherein each metal member has a longitudinal axis and wherein the stamped portion and the longitudinal axis form an acute angle.

7. A blown-in insulation support system for metal frame construction according to claim 6, wherein the stamped portion and the longitudinal axis form an angle of about 20 degrees.

8. A blown-in support system for steel frame construction comprising:
   a nylon net; and
   a steel frame comprising spaced apart steel top and bottom tracks and a plurality of parallel elongate steel studs extending between the top track and the bottom track spaced at intervals along the length of each track, wherein the top track, the bottom track and the elongate studs each have a longitudinal axis and each has at least one portion thereof stamped out to protrude on one side at an angle of about 20 degrees between the protruded portion and the longitudinal axis and an exterior sheath-

6

ing attached to an opposing side, and wherein each stamped out protrusion engages and tensions the nylon net.

9. A method for installing blown-in insulation in metal frame construction, the method comprising the steps of:
   a) providing a metal frame having a plurality of metal members wherein at least two opposing metal members have at least one stamped out portion thereof stamped out to protrude on one side and an exterior sheathing attached to an opposing side;
   b) engaging and tensioning an insulation support material on the stamped out protruded portions of the opposing metal members forming a cavity between the exterior sheathing and the insulation support material; and
   c) blowing insulation into the cavity.

10. A method for installing blown-in insulation in metal frame construction according to claim 9, wherein the metal members are selected from the group consisting of: primary metal members and secondary metal members.

11. A method for installing blown-in insulation in metal frame construction according to claim 10, wherein the primary metal members are selected from the group consisting of: a stud and a joist; and the secondary metal members are selected from the group consisting of: a purlin; a channel; and a track.

12. A method for installing blown-in insulation in metal frame construction according to claim 9, wherein the metal members are formed from steel.

13. A method for installing blown-in insulation in metal frame construction according to claim 12, wherein the metal members are selected from the group consisting of: primary metal members and secondary metal members.

14. A method for installing blown-in insulation in metal frame construction according to claim 13, wherein the primary metal members are selected from the group consisting of: a stud and a joist; and the secondary metal members are selected from the group consisting of: a purlin; a channel; and a track.

15. A method for installing blown-in insulation in metal frame construction according to claim 9, wherein the insulation support material is selected from the group consisting of: a nylon netting; a fabric; a reinforced material; and a thin translucent cloth material for holding insulation.

16. A method for installing blown-in insulation in metal frame construction according to claim 15, wherein the insulation support material is a nylon netting.

17. A method for installing blown-in insulation in metal frame construction according to claim 9, wherein the insulation support material is engaged by hooking the insulation support material on the stamped out protruded portions of the opposing metal members.

18. A method for installing blown-in insulation in steel frame construction, the method comprising the steps of:
   a) providing a steel frame comprising spaced apart steel top and bottom tracks and a plurality of parallel elongate steel studs extending between the top track and the bottom track spaced at intervals along the length of each track, wherein the top track, the bottom track and the elongate studs each have a longitudinal axis and each has at least one portion thereof stamped out to protrude at an angle of about 20 degrees between the protruded portion and the longitudinal axis and an exterior sheathing attached to an opposing side;
   b) hooking and tensioning a nylon net onto the stamped out protruded portions of the steel frame forming a cavity between the exterior sheathing and the nylon net; and
   c) blowing insulation into the cavity.

* * * * *

FIGURE 1.2 *(continues)*

TABLE 1.1

Summary of Intellectual Property Protection

Copyrights	Trademarks	Trade Secrets	Patents
Literary works	Words	Financial information	Machines
Musical works	Slogans	Business information	Articles of manufacture
Dramatic works	Designs	Scientific information	Methods or processes
Pantomimes	Colors	Technical information	Compositions of matter
Choreographic works	Sounds	Economic information	Improvements
Pictorial works	Pictures or other symbols	Engineering information	Plants
Graphic works		Patterns	Ornamental designs
Sculptural works	(The above are used to identify	Plans	
Motion pictures	and distinguish goods.)	Compilations	
Other audiovisual works		Program devices	
Sound recordings		Formulas	
Architectural works		Designs	
		Prototypes	
		Methods, techniques	
		Processes, procedures	
		Programs or codes	
Term: Life of author plus 50 years; Work for hire: Shorter of 75 years from the date of publication or 100 years from date of creation	**Term:** 10 years, renewable in increments of 10 years	**Term:** Until a breach of confidence or discovered by a third party	**Term:** Utility patent, 20 years from filing date; Plant patent, 17 years from issue date; Design patent, 14 years from issue date

from the issue date. The types of patents and patent applications are detailed in Chapter Two.

Review

The first step to protecting an idea is to determine what type of intellectual property will best protect it. Table 1.1 provides a summary of copyright, trademark, trade secret, and patent protection at a glance to help you decide how to protect your idea.

Annotated References

1. 17 U.S.C. §106. *(Statutory definition of a copyright.)*
2. 15 U.S.C. §1127. *(Statutory definition of a trademark.)*
3. 18 U.S.C. §1839. *(Statutory definition of a trade secret.)*
4. 35 U.S.C. §271(a). *(Statutory definition of a patent.)*
5. 15 U.S.C. §§1051-27. *(Portion of the trademark statute known as the Lanham Act.)*
6. 17 U.S.C. §102(a). *(Statutory definition of copyright protection.)*
7. Donald Bruce & Co. v. B.N. Multi Com Corp., No. 96C 8083 (N.D. Ill. May 21, 1997). *(Example of a useful item protected with a copyright.)*
8. Magnussen Furniture, Inc. v. Collezione Europa USA, Inc., No. 96-1917 (4th Cir. June 19, 1997). *(Example of a useful item that was not protectable with a copyright.)*
9. 17 U.S.C. §102(b). *(Statutory definition of what a copyright does not protect.)*
10. Burrow-Giles Lithographic Co. v. Sarony, 111 U.S. 53, 58 (1884). *(Precedent for definition of an author.)*
11. Goldstein v. California, 412 U.S. 546,561, 178 U.S.P.Q. 129, 135 (1973). *(Precedent for definition of an author.)*
12. Community for Creative Non-Violence v. Reid, 490 U.S. 730, 737, 10 U.S.P.Q.2d 1985, 1989 (1989). *(Precedent for definition of an author.)*
13. 17 U.S.C. §201(b). *(Statutory definition of an author of a work made for hire.)*
14. 17 U.S.C. §101. *(Statutory definition of a work made for hire.)*
15. 17 U.S.C. §105. *(Statute relating to copyrights and U.S. government works.)*
16. 17 U.S.C. §501(a). *(Statutory definition of copyright infringement.)*
17. Religious Technology Center v. Lerma, Civ. A. No. 95-1107-A (E.D. Va. Bench order January 19, 1996). *(Example of copyright infringement on the Internet.)*
18. Psihoyos v. Liberation, Inc., No. 96 Civ. 3609 (LMM) (S.D.N.Y. April 30, 1997). *(Example of copyright infringement without a sale of copyrighted material.)*

19. Castle Rock Entertainment v. Carol Publishing Group, 95 Civ. 0775 (SS) (S.D.N.Y. Feb. 27, 1997). *(Example where copyright extends to other media.)*

20. 17 U.S.C. §107. *(Statute relating to the four factors for fair use.)*

21. Golden Dorr, Inc. v. Odisho, 646 F.2d 347, 208 U.S.P.Q. 638 (9th Cir. 1980). *(Precedent for states granting more rights to prevent consumer confusion.)*

22. Tonka Corp. v. Tonk-A-Phone, 805 F.2d 793, 231 U.S.P.Q. 872 (8th Cir. 1986). *(Precedent making it easier to meet the requirements needed to show trademark infringement occurred.)*

23. 15 U.S.C. §1114. *(Statutory definition of trademark infringement.)*

24. P.L. 104-98. *(Trademark infringement under the Federal Trademark Dilution Act.)*

25. Meridian Mutual Insurance Company v. Meridian Insurance Group, Inc., No. 97-1963 (7th Cir. October 29, 1997). *(Example of trademark confusion.)*

26. Hasbro, Inc. v. Internet Entertainment Group, (W.D. Wash. February 5, 1996). *(Example of a trademark that had been tarnished.)*

27. Panavision International L.P. v. Toeppen, No. CV 96-3284 (C.D. Cal. November 1, 1996). *(Example of trademark misuse on the Internet.)*

28. 15 U.S.C. §§1058, 1059. *(Statutory definition of the duration of a trademark registration.)*

29. Dow Chemical Co. v. General Electric Co., No. 97-541-311C2 (Oakland County (MI) Cir. Ct., filed April 1, 1997). *(Example of a potential disclosure of company trade secrets.)*

30. Injection Research Specialists v. Polaris Indus., No. 90-Z-1143 (D. Colo. Jury verdict April 25, 1997). *(Example of trade secret theft.)*

31. Atlas Powder Co. v. E.I. du Pont de Nemours & Co., 750 F.2d 1569, 1580, 224 U.S.P.Q. 409, 416 (Fed. Cir. 1984). *(Example of literal patent infringement.)*

32. Haworth, Inc. v. Steelcase, Inc., No. G-89-30373-CA (W.D. Michigan December 23, 1996). *(Example showing high damage award for patent infringement.)*

2

The Types of Patents and Patent Applications

Once you have established that a patent may protect your idea, the next step is to decide what type or types of patent would best protect it.

U.S. Patents

U.S. patents are applied for and issued through the U.S. Patent and Trademark Office (U.S.P.T.O). The U.S.P.T.O. issues patents for three classes of inventions:

- utility inventions[1] (utility patents)
- ornamental designs[2] (design patents)
- asexually reproduced plants[3] (plant patents)

WARNING: A U.S. patent only provides protection for an invention in the U.S., meaning that one may only exclude others from making, using, selling, offering for sale, or importing the invention in the U.S.

The U.S.P.T.O. will not issue patents for:

(1) inventions specifically excluded by Title 35 of the United States Code (for example, inventions that are a threat to national security);

(2) principles or laws of nature and naturally occurring articles;

(3) inventions requiring only mental activity or mental processes.

Inventions involving mental processes are protected using other forms of intellectual property such as copyrights or trade secrets.

According to the U.S.P.T.O.,[4] the number of patents *applied for* and *issued* has increased every year since 1992. Figure 2.1 shows a comparison of the growth trends for patent application filings and issued patents between 1992 and 1996. The increasing numbers of applications filed and patents granted reflect a general trend toward more people realizing the importance of patent protection.

UTILITY PATENTS

Inventions that function in a unique way to produce a useful result are protected by **utility patents.**

A

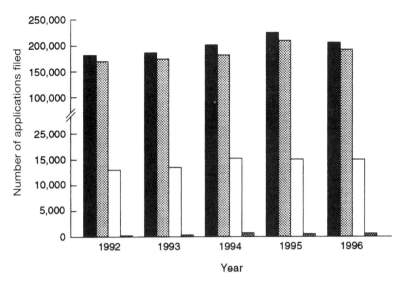

B

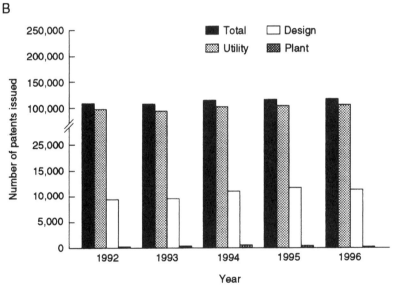

FIGURE 2.1

Growth trends and a comparison of the number of U.S. patents applied for and issued each year. The graph reflects an incremental increase in the number of patents applied for each year with more applications filed in 1995 than in 1996. Note that the patent term changed on June 8, 1995 from 17 years from the issue date to 20 years from the filing date. Many patent practitioners filed applications before June 8, 1995 to obtain the longer of the two patent terms for their clients. The graph also shows that more utility patent applications are filed and issued than design and plant patents.

Utility patents are the most common type of patent issued in the U.S. These patents cover five basic areas of technology: mechanical, electrical, chemical, computer, and biotechnology. In particular, utility patents protect new and useful[5]:

- Machines—devices which accomplish a task and consist of moving parts, like a sewing machine.
- Articles of manufacture—articles produced from raw or prepared materials giving these materials new forms, qualities, properties, or combinations;[6] these articles have no moving parts as their main feature, such as a toothbrush.
- Compositions of matter—chemical compounds or mixtures which give a new form or structure, like a formula for a new glue.
- Processes or methods—inventions involving successive steps where at least one step manipulates some physical object, like the steps in a process for making paint.
- Improvements—to any of the above categories.

All of these *statutory classes* of utility inventions apply to each technology area. However, when claiming inventions in certain technologies, some classes are more suitable than others as shown in Table 2.1.

The majority of the utility patents issue for mechanical inventions. The mechanical arts capture a broad range of devices and gadgets such as toothbrushes or complex machinery. Figure 2.2A shows the front page of a patent for a machine that is used to make a polymeric material that is eventually used in the manufacture of aircraft wings. The abstract describes the parts of the apparatus and how it works. In this example, the invention is defined in terms of a machine and a process. An example of a patent for a mechanical invention that

TABLE 2.1

Common Ways of Claiming Inventions in Various Technologies

Statutory class[a]/ technology	Machine	Article of manufacture	Composition of matter	Process or method
Mechanical	X	X		X
Electrical	X	X		X
Chemical			X	X
Computer	X	X		X
Biotechnology			X	X

[a]Includes improvements.

is protected as an article of manufacture and a method is shown in Fig. 1.2 of Chapter 1.

Electrical utility patents protect electrical inventions. Examples of these types of inventions include electronic circuitry and fiber optics. Figure 2.2B shows the front page of a patent for a fiber optic sensor arrangement. This sensor arrangement is used to measure changes in various physical parameters such as temperature, strain, shape, refractive index, and corrosion. Like the example shown in Fig. 2.2A, the abstract describes the invention as both a machine and a process.

Another common type of utility patent is the chemical utility patent. Chemical patents are primarily directed to compositions of matter and methods more so than to machines or articles of manufacture. The front page of a chemical utility patent is shown in Fig. 2.2C. The abstract shows that the invention is a polyurethane sealant used in horizontal construction joints.

Recent technology advances have led to two new types of inventions that are patentable under the utility classification: computer software and biotechnology inventions. Both of these areas have sparked controversy in the courts with respect to whether these types

A

US005395477A

United States Patent [19]

Sandusky Donald A.

[11] **Patent Number:** **5,395,477**

[45] **Date of Patent:** **Mar. 7, 1995**

[54] **APPARATUS FOR CONSOLIDATING A PRE-IMPREGNATED, FILAMENT-REINFORCED POLYMERIC PREPREG MATERIAL**

[75] Inventor: **Sandusky Donald A.,** Williamsburg, Va.

[73] Assignee: **The United States of America as represented by the Administrator of the National Aeronautics and Space Administration,** Washington, D.C.

[21] Appl. No.: **141,292**

[22] Filed: **Oct. 20, 1993**

[51] Int. Cl.^{6} **B29B 11/16; B29B 15/14; B29K 105/08**

[52] U.S. Cl. **156/441;** 156/180; 156/181; 156/433; 118/124; 264/136; 264/174

[58] Field of Search 156/180, 181, 166, 433, 156/441; 264/136, 174; 425/112, 114; 118/124

[56] **References Cited**

U.S. PATENT DOCUMENTS

2,407,335	9/1946	Wickwire, Jr.	118/124
3,249,484	5/1966	Courtney	156/181 X
3,737,352	6/1973	Avis et al.	156/181
3,993,726	11/1976	Moyer	264/174
4,549,920	10/1985	Cogswell et al.	156/181
4,610,402	9/1986	Corbett et al.	156/425 X
4,626,306	12/1986	Chabner et al.	156/180
4,804,509	2/1989	Angell et al.	264/136
4,919,739	4/1990	Dyksterhouse et al.	156/181
5,094,883	3/1992	Muzzy et al.	427/434.6 X
5,296,064	3/1994	Muzzy et al.	156/180

FOREIGN PATENT DOCUMENTS

550432	3/1993	Japan	156/180
1434926	5/1976	United Kingdom	118/124
422469	9/1974	U.S.S.R.	118/124

Primary Examiner—Jeff H. Aftergut
Attorney, Agent, or Firm—George F. Helfrich; Joy L. Bryant

[57] **ABSTRACT**

An apparatus and method were developed for providing a uniform, consolidated, unidirectional, continuous, fiber-reinforced polymeric material. The apparatus comprises a supply means, a forming means, a shaping means, and a take-up means. The forming means further comprises a pre-melting chamber and a stationary bar assembly. The shaping means is a loaded cooled nip-roller apparatus. Forming takes place by heating a polymeric prepreg material to a temperature where the polymer becomes viscous and applying pressure gradients at separate locations along the prepreg material. Upon exiting the forming means, the polymeric prepreg material is malleable, consolidated and flattened. Shaping takes place by passing the malleable, consolidated, flattened prepreg material through a shaped, matched groove in a loaded, cooled nip-roller apparatus to provide the final solid product.

6 Claims, 5 Drawing Sheets

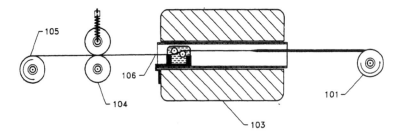

FIGURE 2.2

The front page of a patent for (A) a mechanical, (B) an electrical, (C) a chemical, and (D) a computer software invention. The abstract describes the invention.

B

US005641956A

United States Patent [19]

Vengsarkar et al.

[11] Patent Number: **5,641,956**

[45] Date of Patent: **Jun. 24, 1997**

[54] **OPTICAL WAVEGUIDE SENSOR ARRANGEMENT HAVING GUIDED MODES-NON GUIDED MODES GRATING COUPLER**

[75] Inventors: **Ashish M. Vengsarkar**, Berkeley Heights, N.J.; **Vikram Bhatia**; **Jonathan A. Greene**, both of Blacksburg, Va.; **Kent A. Murphy**, Troutville, Va.

[73] Assignees: **F&S, Inc.**, Blacksburg, Va.; **Lucent Technologies**, Murray Hill, N.J.

[21] Appl. No.: **595,734**

[22] Filed: **Feb. 2, 1996**

[51] Int. Cl.6 .... **H01J 5/16**

[52] U.S. Cl. **250/227.14**; 250/227.24; 385/28

[58] Field of Search 250/227.14, 227.16, 250/227.24, 227.11; 385/28, 37, 50, 32; 356/32; 73/760, 763, 773, 774

[56] **References Cited**

U.S. PATENT DOCUMENTS

4,229,067	10/1980	Love	385/28
4,725,110	2/1988	Glenn et al.	
4,806,012	2/1989	Meltz et al.	356/32
4,950,883	8/1990	Glenn	250/227.14
4,974,931	12/1990	Poole	385/28
4,996,419	2/1991	Morey	250/227.18
5,048,913	9/1991	Glenn et al.	385/37
5,430,817	7/1995	Vengsarkar	385/37

OTHER PUBLICATIONS

T. A. Tran et al., "Real-time immunoassays using fiber optic long-period grating sensors", *Biomedical Sensing, Imaging, and Tracking Technologies I,* Proceedings SPIE—The International Society for Optical Engineering, R.A. Lieberman et al., Eds., vol. 2676, Jan. 29-31, 1996, pp. 165-170.
A. M. Vengsarkar et al., "Long-period fiber gratings as band-rejection filters", *Journal of Lightwave Technology,* vol. 14, No. 1, Jan. 1996, pp. 58-65.

A. M. Vengsarkar et al., "Long-period fiber gratings as gain-flattening and laser stabilizing devices", *Tenth International Conference on Integrated Optics and Optical Fibre Communication,* vol. 5, Jun. 26-30, 1995, pp. 3-4.
A. M. Vengsarkar et al., "Long-period cladding-mode-coupled fiber gratings: Properties and applications", *1995 Technical Digest Series,* vol. 22, Sep. 9-11, 1995, pp. SaB2-1/10-SaB2-4/13.
A. M. Vengsarkar et al., "Long-period fiber gratings as band-rejection filters", *OFC '95,* Feb. 26-Mar. 3, 1995, pp. PD4-1-PD4-5.
V. Bhatia et al., "Optical fiber long-period grating sensors", *Lightnews,* Jan. 1995, pp. 6-11.
F. Bilodeau et al., "Efficient, narrowband LP$_{01}$←→LP$_{02}$ mode converters fabricated in photosensitive fibre: Spectral response", *Electronic Letters,* vol. 27, No. 8, pp. 682-684, Jan. 1991.
K. O. Hill et al., "Efficient mode conversion in telecommunication fibre using externally written gratings", *Electronics Letters,* vol. 26, No. 16, pp. 1270-1272, Aug. 1990.

Primary Examiner—Que Le
Attorney, Agent, or Firm—Joy L. Bryant

[57] **ABSTRACT**

An optical waveguide sensor arrangement for sensing at least one physical parameter is provided. This arrangement comprises an optical waveguide having guided modes, lossy non-guided modes, and a long period grating coupling the guided modes to the lossy non-guided modes wherein the long period grating produces a wavelength transmission spectrum functionally dependent on the physical parameter sensed. A source means provides light to the optical waveguide sensor and an optoelectronic detector, which is positioned in an operable relationship to the optical waveguide sensor, detects light transmitted through the optical waveguide sensor. Lastly, a processing means is attached to the optoelectronic detector for correlating the wavelength transmission spectrum with a numerical value for the physical parameter sensed. The physical parameters sensed by the optical waveguide sensor include: temperature, strain, shape, refractive index and corrosion.

10 Claims, 9 Drawing Sheets

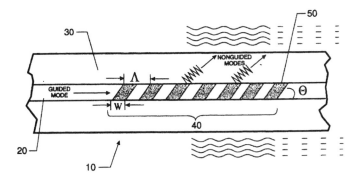

FIGURE 2.2 *(continued)*

C

US005196455A

United States Patent [19]

Bryant

[11]   Patent Number: **5,196,455**

[45]   Date of Patent: **Mar. 23, 1993**

[54]   SELF-LEVELING SEALANT COMPOSITION
         AND METHOD RELATING THERETO

[75]   Inventor: Joy Bryant, Newport News, Va.

[73]   Assignee: Tremco Incorporated, Cleveland,
                      Ohio

[21]   Appl. No.:   707,715

[22]   Filed: May 30, 1991

[51]   Int. Cl.⁵ C08G 18/14
[52]   U.S. Cl. 521/51; 521/110;
         521/126; 521/127; 521/159; 524/730; 528/59
[58]   Field of Search 521/51, 110, 126, 127,
                      521/159; 524/730; 528/59

[56]   References Cited

U.S. PATENT DOCUMENTS

5,004,794 4/1991 Emmerling et al. 528/59

Primary Examiner—Maurice J. Welsh
Attorney, Agent, or Firm—David P. Dureska; Konrad H. Kaeding

[57]   **ABSTRACT**

The present invention relates to a one-part, self-leveling urethane sealant composition for substantially horizontal surfaces, wherein the sealant will flow within a crack, joint or the like and quickly cure to provide an elastomeric seal having a smooth, substantially horizontal surface. The cured sealant provides a surface and volume cure time superior to many known systems, and once cured, provides an elastomeric seal having a superior void volume and void distribution than many known self-leveling sealant systems.

14 Claims, No Drawings

FIGURE 2.2 *(continues)*

of inventions qualify as patentable subject matter. Computer software patents have fallen into a gray area of patentable subject matter because they encompass mental processes and mathematical algorithms, which are not patentable subject matter,[7] per se. Traditionally, software is protected by copyright law. However, the copyright laws do not protect the ideas behind or functions performed by the software. In turn, many software developers found copyright protection to be narrow and undefined. Recent developments in the case law have made it possible to protect computer software programs by patents.[8,9,10,11,12] As with mechanical, electrical, and chemical inventions, computer software inventions may be protected as machines, articles of manufacture, compositions of matter, and/or processes. Software "machines" are defined as specific configurations of discrete hardware elements programmed in a certain way to perform data manipulation functions.[13] A software "article of manufacture" is protectable as a computer memory chip having functional computer software stored on it.[14] A software "composition of matter" is de-

D

US005625816A

United States Patent [19]

Burdick et al.

[11] Patent Number: **5,625,816**

[45] Date of Patent: **Apr. 29, 1997**

[54] **METHOD AND SYSTEM FOR GENERATING PRODUCT PERFORMANCE HISTORY**

[75] Inventors: **Randy Burdick**, Austin, Tex.; **Richard Kittler**, Sunnyvale, Calif.; **F. Walter Smith**, Austin, Tex.

[73] Assignee: **Advanced Micro Devices, Inc.**, Sunnyvale, Calif.

[21] Appl. No.: **223,348**

[22] Filed: **Apr. 5, 1994**

[51] Int. Cl.⁶ **G06F 17/30**

[52] U.S. Cl. 395/614; 364/571.02; 364/489; 379/93; 379/112; 395/210; 395/228

[58] Field of Search 395/600; 379/112, 379/93; 364/489, 580, 401

[56] **References Cited**

U.S. PATENT DOCUMENTS

5,036,479	7/1991	Predais et al.	364/580
5,150,308	9/1992	Hooper et al.	364/489
5,261,094	11/1993	Everson et al.	395/600

5,325,290	6/1994	Cauffman et al.	364/401
5,333,183	7/1994	Herbert	379/112
5,438,614	8/1995	Rozman et al.	379/93

Primary Examiner—Thomas G. Black
Assistant Examiner—Cheryl R. Lewis

[57] **ABSTRACT**

Data in disparate formats from different data sources are reformatted into a common data format and stored in database servers serving one or more data sources such that each database server contains only a portion of the composite database. A client server and graphical user interface are provided for allowing a client to perform simple search requests on one database server, browse requests on all database servers, or serve complex search requests on one or more database servers. The client server may reformat the resultant search data into one or more specific database formats for retrieval and manipulation by a specific database program or display the information for the client. The present invention has particular application to the semiconductor manufacturing field, for tracking data produced during the processes of semiconductor manufacturing.

17 Claims, 23 Drawing Sheets

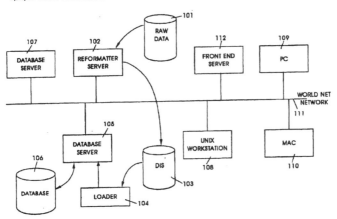

FIGURE 2.2 *(continued)*

scribed as a computer readable medium encoded with information which gives the memory or storage elements contained therein a new form or structure. When the code is acted on by the computer, new qualities or properties result, causing the computer or computer program to function in a practically useful manner.[15] Lastly, computer process inventions include a series of steps that result in a transformation of data or signals, provided that the data or signals represent or constitute physical activity or objects.[16] These examples demonstrate that it is possible to patent computer software using any of the statutory classes, provided that one shows a transformation taking place that involves some form of hardware. A representative example of the front page of a computer software patent is shown in Fig. 2.2D.

Biotechnology inventions involve subject matter relating to life such as transgenic animals, amino acid sequences, or genetic sequences. The patenting of genetically engineered animals has seen its own form of evolution. In *Diamond v. Chakrabarty*[17] the invention was directed toward a genetically engineered bacterium that was capable of breaking down multiple components of crude oil. The court found that the bacterium was patentable either as an article of manufacture or as a composition of matter. Another significant milestone involved the patenting of transgenic mice.[18] The mice were bioengineered to be especially susceptible to contracting cancer and are useful for testing anticancer drugs, as described in the abstract of Fig. 2.3A. Other patents relating to transgenic animals have since issued.

Biotechnology inventions also encompass amino acid and/or genetic sequences. Gene sequence inventions involve cloning. Cloning is the process of isolating and amplifying individual genes from a plant or an animal. Through the cloning process, selected proteins may be readily obtained in large amounts. These proteins might otherwise be scarce or difficult to extract from natural sources. In addition, cloned sequences may also be used for diagnostic purposes such as DNA probes. These inventions have significant commercial value and are typically protected as compositions of matter. Figure 2.3B shows the front page of a patent for a DNA sequence.

To apply for a utility patent a *regular utility patent application* is

A

United States Patent [19]

Leder et al.

[11] Patent Number: **4,736,866**

[45] Date of Patent: **Apr. 12, 1988**

[54] TRANSGENIC NON-HUMAN MAMMALS

[75] Inventors: Philip Leder, Chestnut Hill, Mass.;
Timothy A. Stewart, San Francisco,
Calif.

[73] Assignee: President and Fellows of Harvard
College, Cambridge, Mass.

[21] Appl. No.: 623,774

[22] Filed: Jun. 22, 1984

[51] Int. Cl.⁴ C12N 1/00; C12Q 1/68;
C12N 15/00; C12N 5/00

[52] U.S. Cl. 800/1; 435/6;
435/172.3; 435/240.1; 435/240.2; 435/320;
435/317.1; 935/32; 935/59; 935/70; 935/76;
935/111

[58] Field of Search 435/6, 172.3, 240, 317,
435/320, 240.1, 240.2; 935/70, 76, 59, 111, 32;
800/1

[56] **References Cited**

U.S. PATENT DOCUMENTS

4,535,058 8/1985 Weinberg et al. 435/91
4,579,821 4/1986 Palmiter et al. 435/240

OTHER PUBLICATIONS

Ucker et al, Cell 27:257–266, Dec. 1981.
Ellis et al, Nature 292:506–511, Aug. 1981.
Goldfarb et al, Nature 296:404–409, Apr. 1981.
Huang et al, Cell 27:245–255, Dec. 1981.

Blair et al, Science 212:941–943, 1981.
Der et al, Proc. Natl. Acad. Sci. USA 79:3637–3640,
Jun. 1982.
Shih et al, Cell 29:161–169, 1982.
Gorman et al, Proc. Natl. Acad. Sci. USA
79:6777–6781, Nov. 1982.
Schwab et al, EPA–600/9–82–013, Sym: Carcinogen.
Polynucl. Aromat. Hydrocarbons Mar. Environ.,
212–32 (1982).
Wagner et al. (1981) Proc. Natl. Acad. Sci USA 78,
5016–5020.
Stewart et al. (1982) Science 217, 1046–8.
Costantini et al. (1981) Nature 294, 92–94.
Lacy et al. (1983) Cell 34, 343–358.
McKnight et al. (1983) Cell 34, 335.
Binster et al. (1983) Nature 306, 332–336.
Palmiter et al. (1982) Nature 300, 611–615.
Palmiter et al. (1983) Science 222, 814.
Palmiter et al. (1982) Cell 29, 701–710.

Primary Examiner—Alvin E. Tanenholtz
Attorney, Agent, or Firm—Paul T. Clark

[57] **ABSTRACT**

A transgenic non-human eukaryotic animal whose germ
cells and somatic cells contain an activated oncogene
sequence introduced into the animal, or an ancestor of
the animal, at an embryonic stage.

12 Claims, 2 Drawing Sheets

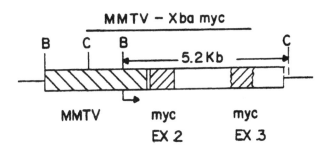

MMTV – Xba myc

FIGURE 2.3 *(continues)*

The front page of a biotechnology patent, issued for (A) a transgenic
nonhuman mammal and (B) a DNA sequence. The abstract describes the
invention.

B

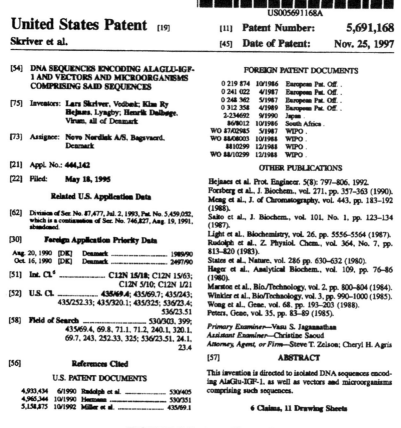

United States Patent [19]

Skriver et al.

[11] Patent Number: 5,691,168

[45] Date of Patent: Nov. 25, 1997

[54] DNA SEQUENCES ENCODING ALAGLU-IGF-1 AND VECTORS AND MICROORGANISMS COMPRISING SAID SEQUENCES

[75] Inventors: **Lars Skriver**, Vedbek; **Kim Ry Hejnaes**, Lyngby; **Henrik Dalbøge**, Virum, all of Denmark

[73] Assignee: **Novo Nordisk A/S**, Bagsvaerd, Denmark

[21] Appl. No.: **444,142**

[22] Filed: **May 18, 1995**

Related U.S. Application Data

[62] Division of Ser. No. 87,477, Jul. 2, 1993, Pat. No. 5,459,052, which is a continuation of Ser. No. 746,827, Aug. 19, 1991, abandoned.

[30] **Foreign Application Priority Data**

Aug. 20, 1990 [DK] Denmark 1989/90
Oct. 16, 1990 [DK] Denmark 2497/90

[51] Int. Cl.⁶ C12N 15/18; C12N 15/63; C12N 5/10; C12N 1/21

[52] U.S. Cl. 435/69.4; 435/69.7; 435/243; 435/252.33; 435/320.1; 435/325; 536/23.4; 536/23.51

[58] Field of Search 530/303, 399; 435/69.4, 69.8, 71.1, 71.2, 240.1, 320.1, 69.7, 243, 252.33, 325; 536/23.51, 24.1, 23.4

[56] **References Cited**

U.S. PATENT DOCUMENTS

4,933,434 6/1990 Rudolph et al. 530/405
4,965,344 10/1990 Hermann 530/351
5,158,875 10/1992 Miller et al. 435/69.1

FOREIGN PATENT DOCUMENTS

0 219 874 10/1986 European Pat. Off. .
0 241 022 4/1987 European Pat. Off. .
0 248 362 5/1987 European Pat. Off. .
0 312 358 4/1989 European Pat. Off. .
2-234692 9/1990 Japan .
86/8012 10/1986 South Africa .
WO 87/02985 5/1987 WIPO .
WO 88/08003 10/1988 WIPO .
8810299 12/1988 WIPO .
WO 88/10299 12/1988 WIPO .

OTHER PUBLICATIONS

Hejnaes et al. Prot. Engineer. 5(8): 797–806, 1992.
Forsberg et al., J. Biochem., vol. 271, pp. 357–363 (1990).
Meng et al., J. of Chromatography, vol. 443, pp. 183–192 (1988).
Saito et al., J. Biochem., vol. 101, No. 1, pp. 123–134 (1987).
Light et al., Biochemistry, vol. 26, pp. 5556–5564 (1987).
Rudolph et al., Z. Physiol. Chem., vol. 364, No. 7, pp. 813–820 (1983).
States et al., Nature, vol. 286 pp. 630–632 (1980).
Hager et al., Analytical Biochem., vol. 109, pp. 76–86 (1980).
Marston et al., Bio./Technology, vol. 2, pp. 800–804 (1984).
Winkler et al., Bio/Technology, vol. 3, pp. 990–1000 (1985).
Wong et al., Gene, vol. 68, pp. 193–203 (1988).
Peters, Gene, vol. 35, pp. 83–89 (1985).

Primary Examiner—Vasu S. Jagannathan
Assistant Examiner—Christine Saoud
Attorney, Agent, or Firm—Steve T. Zelson; Cheryl H. Agris

[57] **ABSTRACT**

This invention is directed to isolated DNA sequences encoding AlaGlu-IGF-1, as well as vectors and microorganisms comprising such sequences.

6 Claims, 11 Drawing Sheets

FIGURE 2.3 *(continued)*

submitted to the U.S.P.T.O. A regular utility patent application contains a *specification,* one or more *drawings* (if necessary), and at least one *claim* defining the invention.

The specification is a description of the invention. It must contain the following three elements:

(1) a *written description* of the invention;

(2) a description of the *best mode* known to the inventor at the time the application is written of how to carry out the invention; and

(3) an *enabling* specification.

Enablement means that the invention is explained well enough in the specification so others may make and use the invention without undergoing undue experimentation.

Not all patent applications require drawings. For example, inventions relating to compositions of matter typically do not have drawings. Conversely, an application for a machine usually has at least one drawing and, more often, a set of drawings.

The claim or claims define the legal limits of the invention. Every regular utility patent application must have at least one claim.

Once the patent is applied for, the application is examined to see if the invention meets the minimum requirements for *novelty*,[19] *utility*,[20] and *nonobviousness*.[21]

Novelty is met if every element in the claimed invention is not found in a single prior patent or publication, or is not generally known to the public.

Utility is met if the invention performs some useful function for society.

Nonobviousness is met if the invention cannot be readily deduced by someone having ordinary skill in the technology based on information that is generally available to the public.

These requirements along with details of how patent applications are prepared, filed, examined and granted are addressed in Chapters 7 and 8. If the invention meets the requirements, the application is allowed and a patent is issued. A utility patent is enforceable for 20 years from the original filing date of the regular patent application.

DESIGN PATENTS

From a patent perspective, a design of an object is the visual characteristics or visual aspects displayed by it. In other words, a design is the appearance of an object which creates a visual impact upon the mind of the observer.[22] A design of an object may encompass:

- its configuration or shape;
- its surface ornamentation; or
- both its shape and surface ornamentation.

A **design patent** merely protects the ornamental aspects of an article or how the article looks.

A design patent does not protect the functional aspects of an invention. In fact, one court found that a design for a body panel for a car was not protectable by a design patent.[23] In this case, the body panel was a fender. The fender was designed based on functional and performance considerations instead of ornamental considerations. Thus, the fender was not entitled to protection by a design patent.

WARNING: A design patent does not protect the functional or useful aspects of a product.

Figure 2.4 shows an example of a design patent for a fiber optic light fixture. A design patent consists of a series of *drawings or photographs* showing the ornamental features of a particular article. The *description* of the invention describes the views of the figures. The U.S.P.T.O. allows only one *claim* that is directed toward the ornamental design for the article as shown and described. Note in the example provided that the fiber optic light fixture is not protected for the way it functions but rather for its unique look.

US00D388198S

United States Patent [19]	[11] Patent Number:	Des. 388,198
Weber	[45] Date of Patent:	**Dec. 23, 1997

[54] **FIBER OPTIC ACCENT LIGHT**

[75] Inventor: **Michael E. Weber**, Blacksburg, Va.

[73] Assignee: **Virginia Tech Intellectual Properties, Inc.**, Blacksburg, Va.

[**] Term: **14 Years**

[21] Appl. No.: **65,001**

[22] Filed: **Jan. 15, 1997**

[51] LOC (6) Cl. **26-05**
[52] U.S. Cl. **D26/27; D26/64; D26/75**
[58] Field of Search 362/147, 404–408, 362/432. 32, 269, 275. 287, 418, 419, 427; D26/60. 62. 63. 65. 64. 66, 27, 75. 76, 77, 78

[56] **References Cited**

U.S. PATENT DOCUMENTS

D. 261,180	10/1981	Lagin	D26/66
4,819,138	4/1989	Polick	362/419
4,821,162	4/1989	Ellis	362/147 X
5,140,508	8/1992	Komonko	362/427 X

OTHER PUBLICATIONS

Author—None (Advertisement). "Design Journal—The Monthly Journal of Design and Architecture". Sep. 1996, p. 20, vol. 9, No. 9, Publishers: John Moses & John Platter, Los Angeles, CA, USA.

Primary Examiner—Susan J. Lucas
Attorney, Agent, or Firm—Joy L. Bryant

[57] **CLAIM**

The ornamental design for a fiber optic accent light, as shown.

DESCRIPTION

FIG. 1 is a perspective view of a fiber optic accent light showing my new design;
FIG. 2 is a bottom view thereof;
FIG. 3 is a top view thereof;
FIG. 4 is a left side view thereof;
FIG. 5 is a rear view thereof;
FIG. 6 is a right side view thereof; and,
FIG. 7 is a front view thereof.

1 Claim, 3 Drawing Sheets

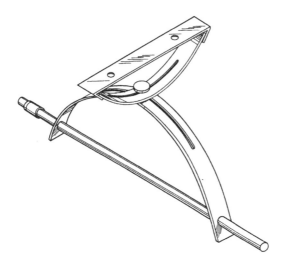

FIGURE 2.4 *(continues)*

A design patent for a fiber optic light fixture. The figures serve as the primary specification for the invention and for interpretation of the claim.

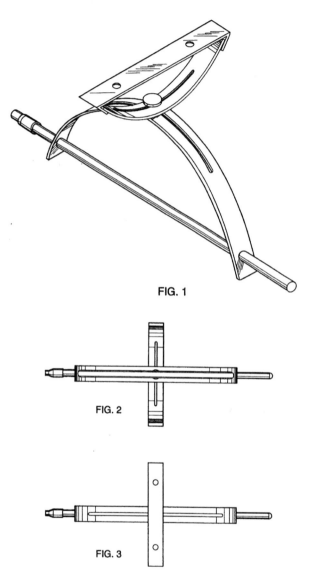

FIG. 1

FIG. 2

FIG. 3

FIGURE 2.4 *(continues)*

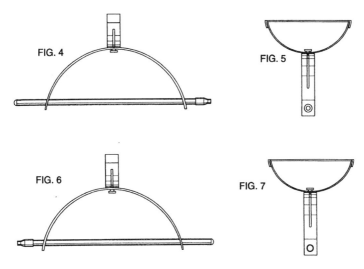

FIGURE 2.4 *(continued)*

It is easy to falsely conclude that design patent applications are simple to prepare, when in fact design patent applications require substantial effort. The details of the design must be taken into consideration and a decision must be made with respect to how much detail is to be included in the drawings. If the drawings include too much detail, then designing around the patent will be easy for a potential infringer. The infringer could simply omit some of the detail and possibly safely operate outside the scope of the patent. Therefore, preparation of a design patent application requires careful thinking, planning, and creativity.

A design patent may be used to protect many kinds of objects. Recently, design patents have been employed to protect computer-generated icons. A design patent application for an icon must show the computer-generated icon on a computer screen, monitor, or other display panel. If the icon is shown standing alone, it is not patentable.[24]

TIP: If your invention is a computer-generated icon, a design patent may protect it. However, you must picture the computer-generated icon on a computer screen or other display.

Once a design patent is submitted to the U.S.P.T.O., it is examined. The design must be *novel* and *nonobvious*. These requirements are met if the shape, configuration, and/or surface ornamentation of the invention is different and not obvious in view of that which is publicly known. If the design is novel and nonobvious, the application is allowed and the design patent issues. Design patents have a term of 14 years from the issue date of the patent.

Note that it is possible to protect an invention with both a design patent and a utility patent. The design patent only protects how the article looks whereas the utility patent protects how it functions. A few examples of inventions that have been protected with both design and utility patents include tire treads, footwear, and flatware.

PLANT PATENTS

Plants are protected in various ways depending on their method of reproduction.

- *Asexually* reproduced plants include those varieties propagated by rooting cuttings, layering, inarching, grafting, budding, or any other method that does not use seeds.
- Plants propagated by seeds are sexually reproduced.

Plant patents protect asexually reproduced plants while sexually reproduced plants are protected under the Plant Variety Protection Act.[25] Both asexually and sexually reproduced plants may also be protected by utility patents.

Plant patents give the owner the right to exclude others from asexually reproducing the plant or selling or using the plant so reproduced.[26]

Plant patents originated in 1930 as a result of the Townsend-Pernell Plant Patent Act. When this Act was established, Congress amended the patent laws to include asexually reproduced plants, other than a tuber-propagated plant or a plant found in an uncultivated state.[27] In turn, plant patents protect:

- distinct and new varieties of plants
- cultivated spores
- mutants
- hybrids
- newly found seedlings

A plant patent is applied for by submitting a plant patent application to the U.S.P.T.O. The plant patent application has a specification and only one claim. The specification gives a complete disclosure of the plant and its distinguishing characteristics. In addition, it includes the origin or parentage of the plant and where and how the plant was asexually reproduced. The claim is directed to the new and distinct variety of the plant which is described and illustrated in the patent application. The claim may also point out certain distinguishing characteristics of the plant.

Surprisingly, a plant patent application is the only type of patent application that must be filed in duplicate. The reason for the duplicate filing is that one copy is submitted to the Department of Agriculture for a report as to whether the plant variety is new and distinct from other plant varieties. When the U.S.P.T.O. receives the application, it is examined. The examiner determines whether the plant variety meets the requirements for patentability: novelty, utility, nonobviousness. If the application is allowed, the plant patent issues.

Plant patent protection is not available for a tuber-propagated plant. Congress intentionally provided this limitation because tuber-propagated plants are propagated by the same part of the plant that one sells as food. The *Manual of Patent Examining Procedure* defines a tuber as meaning a short, thickened portion of an underground branch.[28] Examples of these types of plants include the Irish potato and the Jerusalem artichoke. One way to protect these types of plants is through the Plant Variety Protection Act. This Act permits the U.S. Department of Agriculture to issue a *plant variety certificate.*

> The **Plant Variety Protection Act** grants the owner of a certain sexually reproduced plant the right to exclude others from selling the variety, offering it for sale, reproducing, importing, exporting, or using it in producing (as distinguished from developing) a hybrid or different variety therefrom.[29]

The Plant Variety Protection Act of 1970 was proposed to protect both tuber-propagated plants and sexually reproduced plants. At the time of the Plant Patent Act, new varieties could not be reproduced true-to-type through seedlings. However, by 1970 it was found that this type of reproduction was possible and that some form of plant protection was appropriate.[30]

The Plant Variety Protection Act allows one who breeds or develops sexually reproduced or tuber-propagated plants to be entitled to plant variety protection for the plants. Thus, the Plant Variety Protection Act gives patent-like protection for novel:

- plants grown from seeds

- tuber-propagated plants

Plant variety certificates are not issued by the U.S.P.T.O. Instead, they are issued through the U.S. Department of Agriculture.

There is an exception to the patent-like protection offered by the Plant Variety Protection Act. The Act allows farmers to save enough seed from the protected plants to plant the next year. If the farmer decides not to plant the saved seed, he or she can sell the saved seed to another farmer for planting. However, the amount sold must not exceed the amount needed to seed the seller's field. This exemption only applies to seed that the farmer saved for replanting of the farmer's own acreage. It does not apply to saved seed grown for the purpose of sale.[31] Thus, for seed companies, the Plant Variety Protection Act does not offer as much protection as a patent does. In turn, many seed companies have turned to protecting seeds with utility patents.

> **Utility patents** for plants protect multiple parts of the plant such as seeds, fruit, flowers, cell tissue, transgenes, and transgenic products, and they give the owner the right to exclude others from making, using, selling, offering for sale, or importing the plant or parts of the plant into the U.S.

A utility patent is usually more difficult to obtain for a plant than a plant patent because the rules for utility patents are stricter than those for plant patents. The written description, enablement, and nonobviousness requirements are sometimes difficult to meet for a plant utility invention. Typically, the issue of enablement is satisfied by depositing the seeds in a recognized public depository. The other requirements are usually met by disclosing the significant differences between the claimed plant variety and older varieties.

There are several advantages to protecting a plant by a utility patent instead of a plant patent.

(1) Utility patents may apply to both asexually and sexually reproduced plants.

(2) The utility patent also encompasses multiple varieties, an entire genera or species of a plant.

(3) A utility patent offers coverage for multiple parts of the plant such as seeds or fruit.

(4) Utility patents can contain multiple claims, making it possible to obtain a range of coverage.

An example of a utility patent for a plant invention is shown in Fig. 2.5.

Plant patents are enforceable for 17 years from the issue date. Plants protected under the Plant Variety Protection Act are protected for 20 years whereas plants protected by utility patents are protected for 20 years from the patent application filing date.

Foreign Patents

If foreign protection is desired for an invention, a patent application must be filed, prosecuted, and granted in each country, in that country's language, and in accordance with the requirements of that country. This type of filing is called a *national stage filing*. Filing in many countries can be a costly and time-consuming process. Fortunately, the U.S. participates in several treaties that simplify this process.

The Paris Convention for the Protection of Industrial Property[32] (Paris Convention) resulted from a treaty pertaining to patents and trademarks, in which each member country provides the

US005708189A

United States Patent [19]

Keaschall

[11] Patent Number: **5,708,189**

[45] Date of Patent: ***Jan. 13, 1998**

[54] **INBRED CORN LINE PHP38**

[75] Inventor: **Joseph W. Keaschall**, Sharpsville, Ind.

[73] Assignee: **Pioneer Hi-Bred International, Inc.**, Des Moines, Iowa

[*] Notice: The term of this patent shall not extend beyond the expiration date of Pat. No. 5,506,367.

[21] Appl. No.: **466,683**

[22] Filed: **Jun. 6, 1995**

Related U.S. Application Data

[63] Continuation of Ser. No. 154,939, Nov. 18, 1993, abandoned, which is a continuation of Ser. No. 996,378, Dec. 23, 1992, which is a continuation-in-part of Ser. No. 542,364, Jun. 20, 1990, abandoned.

[51] Int. Cl.[6] A01H 5/00; C12N 5/04
[52] U.S. Cl. **800/200**; 800/250; 800/DIG. 56; 47/58; 47/DIG. 1
[58] Field of Search .... 435/172.3; 47/58, 47/DIG. 1; 800/200, 205, 250, DIG. 56

[56] **References Cited**

U.S. PATENT DOCUMENTS

4,594,810	6/1986	Troyer	47/58
4,812,599	3/1989	Segebart	800/200

FOREIGN PATENT DOCUMENTS

160390 11/1985 European Pat. Off. .

OTHER PUBLICATIONS

Conger, B.V., et al. (1987) "Somatic Embryogenesis From Cultured Leaf Segments of Zea Mays", *Plant Cell Reports*, 6:345–347.

Duncan, D.R., et al. (1985) "The Production of Callus Capable of Plant Regeneration From Immature Embryos of Numerous Zea Mays Genotypes", *Planta*, 165:322–332.

Edallo, et al. (1981) "Chromosomal Variation and Frequency of Spontaneous Mutation Associated with in Vitro Culture and Plant Regeneration in Maize", *Maydica*, XXVI: 39:56.

Green, et al., (1975) "Plant Regeneration From Tissue Cultures of Maize" *Crop Science*, vol. 15, pp. 417–421.

Green, C.E., et al. (1982) "Plant Regeneration in Tissue Cultures of Maize" *Maize for Biological Research*, pp. 367–372.

Hallauer, A.R. et al. (1988) "Corn Breeding" *Corn and Corn Improvement*, No. 18, pp. 463–481.

Meghji, M.R., et al. (1984), "Inbreeding Depression, Inbred & Hybrid Grain Yields, and Other Traits of Maize Genotypes Representing Three Eras", *Crop Science*, vol. 24, pp. 545–549.

Phillips, et al. (1988) "Cell/Tissue Culture and In Vitro Manipulation". *Corn & Corn Improvement*, 3rd Ed., ASA Publication, No. 18, pp. 345–387.

Poehlman (1987) *Breeding Field Crop*, AVI Publication Co., Westport, Ct., pp. 237–246.

Rao, K.V., et al., (1986) "Somatic Embryogenesis in Glume Callus Cultures", *Maize Genetics Cooperative Newsletter*, No. 60, pp. 64–65.

Sass, John F. (1977) "Morphology", *Corn & Corn Improvement*, ASA Publication, Madison, Wisconsin, pp. 89–109.

Songstad, D.D. et al. (1988) "Effect of ACC (1–aminocyclopropane–1–carboxylic acid), Silver Nitrate & Norbonadiene on Plant Regeneration From Maize Callus Cultures", *Plant Cell Reports*, 7:262–265.

Tomes, et al. (1985) "The Effect of Parental Genotype on Initiation of Embryogenic Callus From Elite Maize (*Zea Mays* L.) Germplasm". *Theor. Appl. Genet.*, vol. 70, pp. 505–509.

Troyer, et al. (1985) "Selection for Early Flowering in Corn: 10 Late Synthetics", *Crop Science*, vol. 25, pp. 695–697.

Umbeck, et al. (1983) "Reversion of Male–Sterile T–Cytoplasm Maize to Male Fertility in Tissue Culture", *Crop Science*, vol. 23, pp. 584–588.

Wright, Harold (1980) "Commercial Hybrid Seed Production", *Hybridization of Crop Plants*, Ch. 8: 161–176.

Wych, Robert D. (1988) "Production of Hybrid Seed", *Corn and Corn Improvement*, Ch. 9, pp. 565–607.

Primary Examiner—Gary Benzion
Attorney, Agent, or Firm—Pioneer Hi-Bred International, Inc.

[57] **ABSTRACT**

According to the invention, there is provided an inbred corn line, designated PHP38. This invention thus relates to the plants and seeds of inbred corn line PHP38 and to methods for producing a corn plant produced by crossing the inbred line PHP38 with itself or with another corn plant. This invention further relates to hybrid corn seeds and plants produced by crossing the inbred line PHP38 with another corn line or plant and to crosses with related species.

6 Claims, No Drawings

FIGURE 2.5

Front page of a utility patent for a specific sexually reproduced plant. The abstract describes the invention as a specific inbred corn line coupled with methods for producing the corn plant.

citizens of other member countries the same rights that it gives to its own citizens. Approximately 140 countries follow the Paris Convention, including the U.S. One of the main advantages of the Paris Convention is that it gives an individual the right of *priority* in foreign countries based on an earlier filed application in the person's native country. Priority serves as a way for a person to have his or her native country filing date count as the filing date in a foreign member country if the foreign application is filed within 12 months of the native country application. For example, if a U.S. inventor files a patent application in a foreign member country within 12 months of filing his or her application in the U.S., then the application in the foreign country will be treated as if it were filed on the same day as the U.S. application. This is important because most foreign countries have a *first to file* system. In a first to file system, the first person to file the patent application is the one entitled to the patent.

EXAMPLE

Walt files a patent application for a laser gyroscope in the U.S. on January 3, 1995. On July 3, 1995 (six months after Walt filed his U.S. patent application) Kurt, who is a citizen of Germany, files a patent application in Germany for a laser gyroscope that is similar to Walt's. On November 3, 1995, Walt files a patent application in Germany which is identical to his U.S. patent application. At the time of filing, Walt's patent practitioner advises him that he should claim the benefit of his U.S. filing date in accordance with the Paris Convention. In turn, Walt is accorded the benefit of his earlier U.S. filing date (January 3, 1995) for his German application making him the first to file. This prohibits Kurt from getting a patent in his own country, even though he filed his application on July 3, 1995, ahead of Walt.

_____

WARNING: The U.S. does not have a first to file system.

Another treaty to which the U.S. adheres is the Patent Cooperation Treaty (PCT).[33] This treaty involves more than 90 countries and was enacted in 1978. The PCT provides a central filing procedure and a standardized application format, making it easier to file a patent application for the same invention in foreign member countries in one's native language, delaying the translation requirement. The PCT application is essentially an international patent application. If a PCT application is filed within 12 months of filing an application on the same subject matter in the U.S., the PCT application is entitled to receive the priority date of the originally filed U.S. application. This priority date will be applicable to each country that is designated on the PCT application and one may designate as many PCT member countries as he or she desires. However, in order to obtain a patent in each country, copies of the PCT application will have to be filed in the national patent offices of each country either 20 months or 30 months after the priority date, at which point the application enters the national stage. Note that the PCT applicant may delay entry into the national stage for up to 30 months and to obtain patent protection in a particular foreign country, one must ultimately file a national stage application in that country. Thus, a PCT application serves as an extension of time that allows one to obtain a preliminary search and possibly a preliminary examination without incurring the high costs associated with national stage filings. Therefore, the PCT application is particularly useful for those individuals who are uncertain about where they want patent protection.

The PCT application is filed in a receiving office, such as the U.S.P.T.O. For U.S. inventors to obtain the benefit of their U.S. priority date, the PCT application must be filed within 12 months of the original U.S. patent application filing date. Upon filing the PCT application, the applicant may designate the U.S.P.T.O., or another patent office such as the European Patent Office, as the International Search Authority who conducts a patentability search. The results from this search are usually received within 16 months from the priority date. Often, these search results are used as a basis to change or amend the claims in the application in addition to determining whether the applicant wishes to enter the national stage. The applicant has 2 months from the date the search report is transmitted to amend the claims. The PCT application, the search report, and the amended claims are published 18 months from the priority date. The application enters the national stage 20 months from the priority date. However, this may be further delayed by up to 30 months from the priority date by filing a demand for a preliminary examination within 19 months from the priority date. The demand must designate the countries where the applicant wants the preliminary examination to take place. Upon completion of the preliminary examination, a preliminary examination report issues (approximately 28 months from the priority date) and contains information as to whether the invention is novel, involves an inventive step, and is industrially applicable. At this point, the applicant must decide whether and in which countries to enter the national stage before the expiration of 30 months from the priority date. The preliminary examination report provides useful information for making this decision.

The following example demonstrates the complexity of the PCT process; emphasizes the decisions that must be made during the process; and the timing involved. Because of the complexity of the process, it is advisable to employ the assistance of a patent practitioner when deciding to file a PCT application.

EXAMPLE

Figure 2.6 depicts a time line showing the PCT filing process for the following example.

Anne, an avid cyclist, has invented a new mechanism for controlling the speed of a bicycle and files a U.S. patent application on January 3, 1995. Anne, uncertain of the commercial potential for her bicycle mechanism in Europe and Asia, decides to file a PCT application on December 30, 1995 in the U.S.P.T.O. The PCT application designates all of the European and Asian member countries and also designates the European Patent Office as the International Search Authority.

On May 3, 1996, the search results are received. Based on these results, the claims are amended and filed on June 3, 1996. On July 3, 1996, the PCT application, the search report, and the amended claims are published.

Anne must quickly decide whether she wants to enter the national stage or request international preliminary examination which would further delay entry into the national stage. If Anne decides to delay, a demand must be filed by August 3, 1996 (19 months from the priority date). If Anne decides to enter the national stage, she must do so by September 3, 1996. Anne's investors are not giving her the money she needs to proceed, so Anne decides to delay entrance into the national stage.

A demand for international preliminary examination

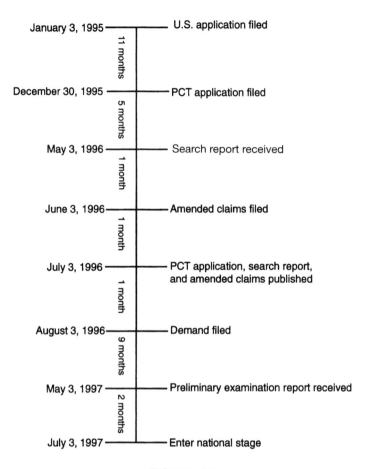

January 3, 1995 ——————— U.S. application filed

11 months

December 30, 1995 ——————— PCT application filed

5 months

May 3, 1996 ——————— Search report received

1 month

June 3, 1996 ——————— Amended claims filed

1 month

July 3, 1996 ——————— PCT application, search report, and amended claims published

1 month

August 3, 1996 ——————— Demand filed

9 months

May 3, 1997 ——————— Preliminary examination report received

2 months

July 3, 1997 ——————— Enter national stage

FIGURE 2.6

Time line representing the PCT filing process and key events occurring in the process. The PCT application must be filed within 12 months of filing in the U.S. in order to obtain the benefit of the priority date. All applications are published 18 months from the priority date and the demand must be filed within 19 months from the priority date to delay entry into the national stage.

is filed on August 3, 1996 electing the countries that showed the most sales potential for Anne's invention. On May 3, 1997, the international preliminary examination report is received. The examiner states that all of the claims are novel, involve an inventive step, and are industrially applicable. Since the report is favorable, Anne's investors come through with the funding needed to complete the requirements for entering the national stage by July 3, 1997.

TIP: If you think you may want patent protection in foreign countries, but you are not sure, file a PCT application designating all the participating countries.

WARNING: A PCT application never issues as a patent. To obtain a patent, a patent application must be translated, filed, and prosecuted in each individual country and fees paid to each country.

PROVISIONAL PATENT APPLICATIONS

A **provisional patent application** is a method of establishing an early priority date of invention by filing a specification describing the invention in the U.S.P.T.O.

A provisional patent application serves as an alternative means to filing a regular patent application in order to obtain a priority date for an invention. A provisional patent application never issues as a patent. Patents only issue from regular applications that are filed in the U.S.P.T.O. However, for a Paris Convention filing or a PCT application, a person may rely on the filing date of the provisional patent application for a priority date.

The provisional patent application became available on June 8, 1995. This type of application resulted from the 1994 Uruguay Round Agreements Act. The reason for implementing a provisional patent application was to put U.S. inventors on an equal ground with foreign inventors with respect to claiming priority. To appreciate the benefit of this, one must realize that the term of a U.S. patent is measured from the filing date of a regular patent application in the U.S., not the priority date of a foreign originated application. Therefore, foreign applicants who claim priority of their patent application filed in their native countries would gain the benefit of having one year in which to file their U.S. application without having it count against their patent term. However, U.S. applicants did not have this benefit because their patent term is calculated from the filing date of their regular U.S. originated patent application. Therefore, the provisional patent application was instituted to provide a priority date without counting against the patent term.

EXAMPLE

Louise files an application in France on January 2, 1996. On December 30, 1996, the U.S. application is filed, claiming the benefit of the French application, filed January 2, 1996. Louise's U.S. patent issues on November 30, 1997. Since the patent expiration date is calculated based on the U.S. filing date, the patent will expire on December 30, 2016.

Jesse, a U.S. citizen, files his regular patent application in the U.S. on January 2, 1996. His U.S. patent issues on November 30, 1997. The term of Jesse's patent is measured from January 2, 1996. Therefore, Jesse's patent will expire on January 2, 2016, almost one whole year before Louise's patent expires.

Hillary, a U.S. citizen, files a provisional patent application in the U.S. on January 2, 1996. On December 30, 1996, she files a regular patent application in the U.S., claiming the benefit of the priority date of the provisional patent application. Hillary's patent issues on November 30, 1997. Her patent will expire on December 30, 2016 the same time as Louise's patent expires, which is almost one whole year after Jesse's patent expires.

It is important to realize that one cannot claim the benefit of a priority date based on a provisional patent application when filing a design patent application.[34] In addition, a regular utility patent application must be filed within 1 year of the filing date of the provisional patent application or the priority date will be lost.

WARNING: The priority date based on a provisional patent application cannot be applied to a design patent application.

WARNING: In order to maintain the benefit of the priority date of the provisional patent application, a regular patent application must be filed within 1 year of the filing date of the provisional patent application.

Provisional applications offer several other advantages besides securing the benefit of a priority date in the U.S. The requirements for preparing a provisional patent application are not as strict as the requirements for a regular application. The U.S.P.T.O. does not require a provisional application to have claims. However, the application must contain a description of the invention, be enabling, and show the best mode in order to obtain the benefit of the priority date. In addition, the filing fee for a provisional patent application is only a fraction of the filing fee for a regular patent application.

There are several circumstances that dictate when a provisional patent application should be filed. One instance may be if the inventor knows that he or she may be publishing the invention and there is not enough time to prepare a regular patent application. This is common in academia. Another time to file the provisional application is if one wants to test market the invention, or raise venture capital. The provisional application would provide the applicant with a 1 year grace period to sell the invention without jeopardizing foreign filing rights or affecting the patent term. A provisional application may also be filed to obtain the earliest possible filing date in the U.S.P.T.O. This date is especially useful if one suspects that someone else may be working on the same invention and may file a patent application for it (problems associated with this event are explained in Chapter 3). Lastly, a provisional application serves as a *constructive reduction to practice*. Constructive reduction to practice is a way of reducing an invention to practice without physically making or practicing the invention. It is accomplished by filing a patent application in the U.S.P.T.O. that adequately discloses the invention by providing a description written in the present tense. Many people refer to these types of patent applications or the patents that issue from them as *paper patents*. A constructive reduction to practice serves as a vehicle for claiming an invention if it cannot be actually reduced to practice due to a lack of resources or other necessary means.

TIP: If you don't have enough time to prepare a regular U.S. patent application, file a provisional patent application.

TIP: If you want to test market your invention before

entering the patent process and still protect your foreign filing rights, file a provisional application first.

TIP: If you do not have the resources to make the invention, file a provisional patent application and have it serve as a constructive reduction to practice.

There are several disadvantages to filing a provisional patent application. Filing a provisional patent application delays a patent issuing by possibly as much as one year. The overall cost of patenting is higher because of the extra fees associated with the preparation and filing of the provisional patent application. Filing a provisional patent application starts the 1-year period in which a foreign application must be filed. In turn, a foreign application may have to be filed at the same time as the regular U.S. application. If the invention is not properly disclosed in the provisional application and new information must be added to the regular patent application, the new information will not be entitled to the priority date of the provisional application. Table 2.2 summarizes the pros and cons of filing a provisional application.

WARNING: A provisional patent application never issues as a patent. To get a patent, one must file a regular patent application in the U.S.P.T.O.

Review

Some inventions may be protected using two types of patents while other inventions may not seem to be patentable at all. For example, silverware or flatware may be patentable as both an ornamental design and a utility invention. Conversely, an invention for a sex-

TABLE 2.2

The Pros and Cons of Filing a Provisional Patent Application

Pros	Cons
Enables the earliest possible filing date without adversely affecting the patent term	Never issues as a patent
Allows test marketing of the invention while having an early filing date	Delays issuance of the patent by up to 1 year
Less formal application requirements	Added expense of preparing and filing the application
Can be filed quickly	Risks inadequate disclosure of the invention
U.S.P.T.O. filing fee is a fraction of the fee for regular application	Starts the 1-year period in which a foreign application must be filed
Serves as a constructive reduction to practice	

ually reproduced plant or a tuber propagated plant is not protectable as a plant patent but may be protected through the Plant Variety Protection Act or as a utility patent. U.S. patents provide protection only in the U.S. To obtain foreign protection, a patent application must be filed in each individual country in the language of and according to the laws of that country.

The provisional patent application and the PCT application are two types of patent applications that may be filed to get a priority date. These applications never issue as patents but serve as extensions of time for filing regular patent applications. Having the earliest possible filing date is beneficial for those countries having a first to file system or if you suspect that someone else is working on the same invention and might patent it before you.

Annotated References

1. 35 U.S.C. §101. *(Statute relating to utility patents.)*
2. 35 U.S.C. §171. *(Statute relating to design patents.)*
3. 35 U.S.C. §161. *(Statute relating to plant patents.)*
4. U.S.P.T.O. 1996 Annual Report. *(Statistics on patent application filings and patents issued.)*
5. 35 U.S.C. §101.
6. Diamond v. Chakrabarty, 447 U.S. 303, 308 (1980). *(Defines article of manufacture.)*
7. Diamond v. Diehr, 450 U.S. 175 (1981). *(Defines mental processes as not patentable.)*
8. In re Schrader, 22 F.3d 290 (Fed. Cir. 1994). *(Precedent for computer software patents.)*
9. In re Alappat, 33 F.3d 1526 (Fed. Cir. 1994). *(Precedent for computer software patents.)*
10. In re Warmerdam, 33 F.3d 1354 (Fed. Cir. 1994). *(Precedent for computer software patents.)*
11. In re Lowry, 32 F.3d 1579 (Fed. Cir. 1994). *(Precedent for computer software patents.)*
12. In re Trovato, 42 F.3d 1376 (Fed. Cir. 1994). *(Precedent for computer software patents.)*
13. In re Alappat, 33 F.3d 1526 (Fed. Cir. 1994). *(Defines software in terms of a machine.)*
14. In re Beauregard, No. 95-1054. *(Defines software in terms of an article of manufacture.)*
15. In re Lowry, 32 F.3d 1579 (Fed. Cir. 1994). *(Defines software in terms of composition of matter.)*
16. In re Schrader, 22 F.3d 290 (Fed. Cir. 1994). *(Defines software in terms of a process.)*
17. Diamond v. Chakrabarty, 447 U.S. 303, 206 U.S.P.Q. 193 (1980).
18. U.S. patent No. 4,736,866. *(Patent for a transgenic mouse.)*
19. 35 U.S.C. §102. *(Statutory definition for novelty.)*
20. 35 U.S.C. §101. *(Statutory definition for utility.)*
21. 35 U.S.C. §103. *(Statutory definition for nonobviousness.)*
22. Manual of Patent Examining Procedure section 1502. *(Definition of a design.)*
23. Chrysler Motors Corp. v. Auto Body Panels of Ohio, 12 USPQ2d 1493 (S.D. Ohio 1989). *(Precedent for design patent not protecting functional features of an invention.)*
24. Manual of Patent Examining Procedure section 1504.01A1(a). *(How to patent computer-generated icons.)*
25. 7 U.S.C.§2483(a)(1). *(Plant Variety Protection Act.)*

26. 35 U.S.C. §163. *(Statutory definition of a plant patent.)*

27. 35 U.S.C. §161. *(Statutory definition of a plant.)*

28. Manual of Patent Examining Procedure section 1601. *(Definition of a tuber.)*

29. 7 U.S.C. §2483(a)(1).

30. Diamond v. Chakrabarty, 447 U.S. 303, 313, 206 USPQ 193, 199 (1980). *(Plant patent protection.)*

31. Asgrow Seed Co. v. Winterboer, 115 S. Ct. 788, 33 USPQ2d 1430 (1995). *(Exception to Plant Variety Protection Act.)*

32. McCarthy, J. Thomas (1996). *In* "McCarthy's Desk Encyclopedia of Intellectual Property," 2nd ed., p. 309. BNA Books, Washington, DC. *(Paris Convention for the Protection of Industrial Property.)*

33. McCarthy, J. Thomas (1996). *In* "McCarthy's Desk Encyclopedia of Intellectual Property," 2nd ed., pp. 314—316. BNA Books, Washington, DC. *(Patent Cooperation Treaty.)*

34. 37 C.F.R. §1.78(a)(3). *(Rule stating that a design application may not claim priority based on a provisional application.)*

3

The Invention Process

The U.S. is a first to invent country. Therefore, in order to obtain a patent in the U.S., you must be able to show that you were the first to invent. This chapter explains the invention process with respect to U.S. patent law.

What Is the Invention Process?

The invention process begins when a person has identified and solved a particular problem. Merely identifying a problem does not constitute invention. In fact, an inventor of a particular technology may not necessarily be the one who initially identifies the problem.

In industry, the marketing group often identifies problems. In academia, those who are working in a particular field may identify problems. For individuals, friends or family members are sometimes the ones who identify problems.

EXAMPLE

Bary Bertiger and his wife were on vacation in the Bahamas. Bary's wife tried to place a cellular phone call from the Bahamas back to her home in the U.S. When she was having trouble, she asked a simple question, "Why can't a smart guy like you make my phone work?" This question started Bary Bertiger on an 11-year quest to make a satellite-based wireless telephone system. This system is Motorola's "Iridium Project" and is expected to earn $2.5 billion in annual revenue starting in the year 2000.[1] In this example, it was not his wife's identification of the problem that is considered the invention, but Bary Bertiger's solution.

An invention results when new ideas are executed by some physical means. During the invention process, emphasis is placed on the method of solving the problem. This process encompasses four events:

(1) conception

(2) reduction to practice

(3) diligence

(4) filing a patent application

The **inventive process** begins with conception and ends with a reduction to practice.

CONCEPTION

Conception occurs when an inventor formulates in his or her mind a specific method of solving a problem or achieving a result.

For conception to occur, the inventor must have worked out all of the details to practice the invention. Thus, to constitute conception in patent law, Bary Bertiger's idea to make a satellite-based wireless telephone system had to be thought out in enough detail to accomplish the invention.

To prove conception in court, there must be independent corroborating evidence that shows the inventor revealed to others the "completed thought expressed in such clear terms as to enable those skilled in the art" to make the invention. Corroboration is required. This requirement necessitates that there be a witness who is a non-inventor and can testify that he or she had knowledge of and understood the inventor's concept at the time conception is alleged.[2]

> *WARNING:* Mailing a letter to yourself via registered mail does not provide the corroboration needed to prove that you conceived of the invention on a particular date.

A good witness is one who is technically competent in the field of the invention and is not a coinventor. Technical competency is necessary because the witness may have to testify to various facts surrounding the nature and subject matter of the invention.

TIP: Choose a witness who is technically competent in the field of the invention but is not a coinventor.

REDUCTION TO PRACTICE

After conception has occurred, the only step left is to construct the invention.[3,4] This construction results in the invention being *reduced to practice.*

> **Reduction to practice** completes the inventive process. It is the part of the process that produces an invention.
>
> **Actual reduction to practice** occurs when the invention is physically constructed and it works for its intended purpose. If the invention is a process, then the steps of the process must be carried out.
>
> **Constructive reduction to practice** does not involve the physical construction of the invention. It is the filing of a patent application that adequately discloses the invention in the U.S. Patent and Trademark Office (U.S.P.T.O.).

For actual reduction to practice to occur, the invention must contain all of the elements that define it. Once the invention is constructed, it must be tested to reasonably show that it works or accomplishes its intended use. This type of testing is often referred to as *experimental use* of the invention. When the last test to show operability is completed, actual reduction to practice occurs. Thus, actual reduction to practice is established at a particular point in time when the inventor is able to show that the invention works.

Constructive reduction to practice does not involve any physical construction of the invention. Instead, one files a patent application that adequately discloses the invention in the U.S.P.T.O. The patent that results from this type of filing is often referred to as a *paper patent* or *concept patent*. Any number of reasons may dictate why one would opt for a constructive reduction to practice instead of an actual reduction to practice. One common reason is that the inventor does not have the money to make the invention. Another reason may be that the facilities or materials needed to construct the invention are not readily available. A problem associated with a constructive reduction to practice is that the only reliable date for the reduction to practice is the patent application filing date.

DILIGENCE

Certain circumstances require the inventor to prove that he or she was *diligent* in reducing the invention to practice from the date of conception. This becomes necessary when the inventor is the first to conceive of the invention but is second to reduce it to practice either actually or constructively. In this instance, the inventor must show diligence from the date prior to the second party's conception, to the date prior to the inventor's actual or constructive reduction to practice. The diligence must be a continual effort to make the invention (actual reduction to practice) or file the patent application in the U.S.P.T.O. (constructive reduction to practice). Diligence does not need to be shown when a party is the first to conceive and the first to reduce the invention to practice.

Diligence is defined as the continuous inventive activity by the inventor who was first to conceive of the invention but last to reduce the invention to practice.[5]

The United States: A First to Invent Country

Since the U.S. is a first to invent country, a patent is granted to the person who can prove that he or she was the first to invent. This differs significantly from most countries where the patent is awarded to the first person who files a patent application. When a person can prove that he or she was the first to invent, *priority of invention* is established.

> **Priority of invention** is awarded to the one who can prove that he or she was the first to invent. The inventor with priority of invention is granted the patent.

Although the U.S. does not have a first to file system, having the earliest possible filing date is still important. The advantage to this is realized when two or more parties claim the same invention. When this event occurs, an interference is declared.

> An **interference** is an administrative proceeding that takes place in the U.S.P.T.O. During this proceeding, the Board of Patent Appeals and Interferences must determine who was the first to invent. The one who can prove priority of invention is entitled to the patent.

The party having the earliest possible filing date is awarded senior party status. This status places the burden of providing evidence of an earlier date of invention on the other party, or the junior party. In order to win the interference, the inventor must show the earliest date of conception and reduction to practice. In addition, the inventor may need to provide evidence that he or she was diligent in reducing the invention to practice and subsequently preparing and filing a patent application in the U.S.P.T.O. There are three ways in which a party may win an interference:

(1) by being the first to conceive and the first to reduce to practice;

(2) by being the first to conceive and the last to reduce to practice, coupled with diligence; and

(3) by being second to conceive but first to reduce to practice where the other party was *not* diligent in reducing the invention to practice.

Figure 3.1 and the following example demonstrates the third scenario.

EXAMPLE

Chet conceived of a new watch mechanism on February 3, 1995. However, due to financial constraints and personal obligations he was not able to begin working on the invention until December 1, 1995. From December 1, 1995 until February 3, 1996, Chet worked continuously on the new watch mechanism. On February 3, 1996, he had completed testing on the mechanism. On March 3, 1996, Chet filed his patent application in the U.S.P.T.O., claiming the mechanism.

Fred conceived of a new watch mechanism that was similar to Chet's, on July 3, 1995. Fred was so excited about his idea that he immediately went to work on a prototype. By November 1, 1995, Fred had completed testing on the mechanism. On January 3, 1996, Fred filed his patent application in the U.S.P.T.O., claiming the mechanism.

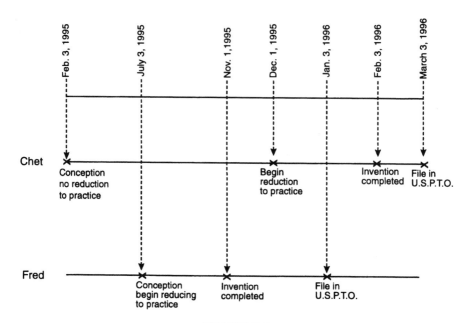

FIGURE 3.1

Time line depicting how Fred won an interference even though he was second to conceive of the invention. Chet's inactivity between his date of conception and the date he began to actually reduce his invention to practice caused him to lose the interference.

An interference was declared between Chet and Fred's applications. Since Fred filed his patent application before Chet, Fred had senior party status. The burden was on Chet to prove that he had conceived of his invention at an earlier date than Fred and that he was diligent in reducing the invention to practice. Chet, having a date of conception of February 3, 1995, clearly had Fred beat on the conception date. However, since Chet delayed in working on the invention until December 1, 1995 and did not complete the invention until February 3, 1996, he was not diligent. Thus, Fred wins the interference.

Proving Conception, Reduction to Practice, and Diligence

The key to winning an interference is being able to provide evidence of all three stages: conception, reduction to practice, and diligence. As noted earlier, one way to prove conception is by having a witness. However, having a witness in combination with some form of documentation is best. An inventor may document conception by the following two methods:

(1) U.S.P.T.O. Disclosure Document Program

(2) Laboratory notebooks

U.S.P.T.O. DISCLOSURE DOCUMENT PROGRAM

The U.S.P.T.O.'s Disclosure Document Program is a service where the U.S.P.T.O. serves as the witness for conception. To take advantage of this service, one simply prepares a paper revealing the invention, a Disclosure Document, and mails the document along with the appropriate fee to the U.S.P.T.O. Once they receive the Disclosure Document, it is kept in confidence for 2 years. If the inventor refers to the document in a patent application, it is kept until the patent expires.

A **Disclosure Document** is a paper revealing the invention that is sent by the inventor to the U.S.P.T.O.

Although, initially this program sounds like a good alternative to having a witness, there are several problems associated with it. One problem is that the document is only kept for 2 years. Thus, if it takes the inventor more than 2 years to reduce the invention to practice, the patent office has destroyed the document and the evidence of conception. Secondly, inventors often misconstrue the Disclosure Document Program as a way to obtain a grace period before filing a regular patent application. In fact, filing a Disclosure Document and waiting to file a patent application until the last possible date, with no reason for such a wait, causes the document to serve as proof of lack of diligence. Lastly, some inventors mistake the Disclosure Document Program as a substitution for filing a patent application. The Disclosure Document is not a patent application and does not give the inventor any patent protection.

> *TIP:* If you do not want to reveal your invention to another person, you may file a Disclosure Document and have the U.S.P.T.O. document your date of conception.

> *WARNING:* (1) The Disclosure Document is kept for only 2 years.
> (2) Filing a Disclosure Document does not grant a 2 year grace period before a patent application must be filed.
> (3) The Disclosure Document does not provide any patent protection.

LABORATORY NOTEBOOKS

The laboratory notebook is a good alternative to the Disclosure Document Program. Not only may it be used to document conception, but it may also be employed to document diligence and reduction to practice. The importance of laboratory notebooks and how to keep them are detailed in Chapter 4.

Review

The invention process involves conception, reduction to practice, diligence, and filing a patent application in the U.S.P.T.O. For conception to occur, the inventor must have all the details of the invention worked out in his or her mind. These details need to be documented and corroborated by a witness. After conception, the inventor must work diligently to reduce the invention to practice and file a patent application in the U.S.P.T.O. If two parties claim the same invention in a patent application or an issued patent and a patent application, the patent will only be awarded to the party that can prove it was the first to invent. Therefore, documenting the circumstances surrounding conception, reduction to practice, and diligence is a very important part of the U.S. patent process.

Annotated References

1. Quentin Hardy, "Higher Calling: How a Wife's Question Led Motorola to Chase Global Cell-Phone Plan," *The Wall Street Journal*, December 16, 1996. *(Example of conception.)*
2. Coleman v. Dines, 754 F.2d 353, 359, 224 U.S.P.Q. 857, 862 (Fed. Cir. 1985). *(Emphasizes the importance of having corroborating evidence of conception.)*
3. Mergenthaler v. Scudder, 11 App. D.C. 264, 276, 1987 C.D. 724, 731 (1897). *(Sets precedent for construction being the only thing left after conception.)*
4. Gunter v. Stream, 573 F.2d 77, 80, 197 U.S.P.Q. 482-484 (C.C.P.A. 1978). *(Sets precedent for construction being the only thing left after conception.)*
5. McCarthy, J. Thomas (1996). *In* "McCarthy's Desk Encyclopedia of Intellectual Property," 2nd ed., pp. 314–316. BNA Books, Washington, DC. *(Definition of diligence.)*

4

Documenting Your Ideas

$\mathbf{P}$erhaps one of the most important things you could do to protect your idea is to document it. This is done by obtaining and maintaining a laboratory notebook throughout the invention process.

Laboratory Notebooks

Laboratory notebooks serve as a very important form of documentation for an invention. They are used to document not only conception but the whole invention process. The notebook is the property of the entity that distributes it. Thus, if a company gives each employee a notebook, it is understood that the notebook belongs to the company and it is to remain with the company when the employee leaves. This has caused problems in the past because many employees view the notebooks as their own property. A big problem occurs when employment is terminated and the employee takes the notebook. Not only does the company lose the information contained in the notebook, but the former employee may have committed trade secret theft by taking the notebook. Another common mistake is for an individual to record his or her "garage" invention in a company notebook. The "garage" invention now becomes the property of the company.

> *TIP:* Your laboratory notebook is only your property if you purchased it. Therefore, purchase your own laboratory notebook if you are inventing on your own.

Keeping a Laboratory Notebook

There are certain guidelines for keeping a laboratory notebook. One of the main requirements is that it must be bound, meaning the pages are sewn into the binding. Spiral notebooks or books with perforated pages are not acceptable because one can remove the pages. Removing pages and altering or fabricating data are all considered fraudulent activities and should be avoided. Most companies supply their researchers with notebooks. Institutions of higher education typically sell lab notebooks in their bookstores. Individual inventors may purchase notebooks from a university bookstore, through the Internet (see Appendix I), or from an office supply store. Although office supply stores do not carry laboratory notebooks, per se, a Mead brand composition notebook is acceptable.

Use of electronic notebooks has become more frequent. To date, the U.S.P.T.O. and the courts have not determined whether electronic notebooks are acceptable as evidence. However, some members of industry have formed an electronic notebook consortium to influence the creation and design of software and standards for R&D and testing lab applications. Perhaps, within the next decade, electronic notebooks will be accepted.

The first several pages of the notebook should be left blank to allow for a table of contents. An inventor should number and title all pages of the notebook. When an individual has an idea, he or she should enter it into the notebook in as much detail as possible using a permanent, black ink, ball point pen. Black ball point ink is preferred because:

(1) it does not smear or run;

(2) it does not fade; and

(3) it photocopies well.

All entries should be made during the course of experimentation and not after the fact. If an error or change must be made, a single line is drawn through the error, initialed, and dated. For larger errors, an "x" may be used to delete the data or any remaining white or blank space on a page. Liquid paper should never be used in the lab notebook.

The inventor should sign and date the bottom of each page on the date of entry. The entries should not be back-dated as this is construed by the courts as fraud. At least one witness, who is not personally involved with the invention, should sign and date each page. Ideally, the witness should sign the page on the same date the entry was made. However, if this is not possible, the notebook should be witnessed as soon as possible since delays may cause problems. For example, an entry made by an inventor in January and witnessed in July may only establish a date of July for the entry. Figure 4.1 shows an exemplary page from a laboratory notebook that has been correctly completed.

| Continued From Page ___ | Title Cherry-Chocolate Chip Cookie Recipe | Continued On Page ___ |

Purpose: To make a cherry-chocolate chip cookie.

Procedure:
In a mixing bowl blend: 2 sticks margarine (softened)
3/4 cup white sugar
3/4 cup brown sugar

Mixed 2 minutes until creamy.

Add to mixture: 1/2 tsp cherry juice
2 eggs

Mixed 2 minutes until well-blended

Add to mixture: 1/2 tsp baking soda
2 1/2 cups flour

Mixed 3 minutes to a dough-like consistency.

Add to dough: 2 cups chocolate chips
1/2 cup maraschino cherries

Mixed until well blended.

Heat oven to 375°F.
Drop dough onto cookie sheet.
Bake at 375°F for 8-10 minutes.
Let cool on wire rack.

Results:
Cookies burned ~~in~~ MG 2-4-68 near cherries.
Tasted too sweet.

Conclusions:
~~Enc~~ MG 2-4-68   Reduce cherry content.
Reduce sugar content.

MG 2-4-68

| Signature M. Good | Date 2-4-68 | Witnessed and understood by me. Yum-mie Signature Date 2-4-68 Yum-mie Name (Print) |

FIGURE 4.1

Sample page from a laboratory notebook. The page contains a title, purpose, experimental procedure, and results section. A line has been drawn through all mistakes and all blank spaces marked out with an "x" followed by the inventor's initials. The page was signed and witnessed on the date the entry was made.

TIP: Set aside time each day to sign your laboratory notebook and have it witnessed at least once a week.

The Business and Legal Reasons for Keeping a Notebook

There are both business reasons and legal reasons for keeping a notebook. For the industrial inventor, a lab notebook serves as a historical record for the company. It reflects the projects which the company pursued during different times in its history and gives a historical record of the company's various product lines. The lab notebook may also be relied upon by the company for:

(1) government audits when federal funding is involved;

(2) Food and Drug Administration (FDA) audits;

(3) Internal Revenue Service (IRS) audits;

(4) product liability lawsuits; and

(5) establishing proof that the company was in possession of a particular trade secret.

For the academic researcher, a laboratory notebook serves as a record from which work can be reproduced. When a Master's or Doctoral candidate has completed his or her degree, another student may continue the research project. Leaving behind a well-documented account of the research work serves as a foundation for further research.

The laboratory notebook provides a way for an individual inventor to organize and document his or her thoughts. It documents what has been tested. It also helps the inventor identify the experiments that were successes and failures. This type of documentation acts as a road map for charting a course for future research.

Laboratory notebooks become very important during patent proceedings. The patent process may be viewed as a two-part process:

(1) *patent prosecution*—obtaining the patent; and

(2) *patent litigation*—enforcing the patent.

One issue that may arise during patent prosecution is an interference proceeding. If there is an interference, it will be necessary to prove the earliest date of conception and reduction to practice. In addition, one may have to show that he or she was diligent in reducing the invention to practice. This type of evidence is typically found in the laboratory notebook. Another issue that arises during patent prosecution relates to *references* and *statutory bars*.

A **reference** is any printed patent, printed publication, or previously known subject matter that may be used to determine the patentability of an invention.

A **statutory bar** is an act defined by the law that, if committed, may prevent a person from obtaining a patent if the patent application is not filed within 1 year from the time the act was committed.

In the U.S., an inventor is granted a 1-year grace period from the time the invention is made public, in which to file a patent application. If a patent application is filed before the expiration of the 1-year grace period, the applicant is not "barred" from patenting. For example, suppose an article is published for an invention. Another inventor, not the author, files a patent application claiming the invention within the 1-year grace period. Most likely, the inventor will have to prove a date of invention prior to the publication date of the reference. One way this is accomplished is by supplying an affidavit along with pages from the lab notebook showing that the inventor had possession of the invention before the date of the reference. This scenario is common in academic and federal laboratory environments where emphasis is placed on having a large number of publications.

The laboratory notebook also serves as a useful tool for determining inventorship. If the wrong inventors are named on a patent, the patent is not valid. Thus, most patent practitioners make it a point to check with all the individuals involved on a project to determine the correct inventorship. The lab notebooks from each individual should reflect each contribution to the project. Inventorship is often disputed in the academic environment where a student, who is working under the direction of an advisor, may think that he or she is an inventor. The dispute is typically resolved by reviewing the laboratory notebooks.

When there is a question of patent infringement, the laboratory notebook serves as a key piece of evidence. Invalidating a patent is a defense to infringement. Two ways to invalidate a patent include:

(1) proving that the inventorship is incorrect; and

(2) showing that the inventor abandoned the invention.

Incorrect inventorship typically occurs in either the corporate environment or the academic environment. It is a common practice in the scientific community to incorporate the names of all the individuals involved in a project on any publications, reports, or papers that may result from the project. Although this practice is acceptable in the scientific community, it cannot be carried over to patent practice. If this occurs, the patent may be invalidated by proving that a particular individual or individuals did not contribute to the claimed invention. Conversely, a patent can also be invalidated if an inventor is omitted.

TIP: Everyone, including management, should keep a laboratory notebook for recording his or her contributions to a particular project.

A hidden disadvantage to keeping a laboratory notebook is that it can be used against the inventor. If a person has an idea, records it in the laboratory notebook, and does not immediately begin working on it to reduce it to practice, then the laboratory notebook will serve as evidence showing a lack of diligence. What is worse than a lack of diligence is a case of documented *abandonment.* This occurs when an individual has an idea for an invention, begins working on it, discontinues working on it, and then picks the project up several months or years later. The unaccounted time between conception and reduction to practice is construed as abandonment. In this instance, the abandonment is documented. If a project must be suspended for a length of time, an entry should be made in the notebook indicating a reason for the suspension.

WARNING: Information contained in a laboratory notebook is discoverable in litigation and may be used to invalidate a patent.

Review

The advantages of having a laboratory notebook far outweigh the disadvantages and the reasons for keeping a laboratory notebook are numerous. However, the laboratory notebook is only useful if the entries are made and witnessed properly. The rules shown in Table 4.1 provide some general guidelines on how to properly record an invention in a laboratory notebook.

TABLE 4.1

Rules for Good Record Keeping

1. Keep all records in a bound notebook.

2. Mark all entries in black ball point ink.

3. Sign and date each notebook page on the date of entry. (*Do not back-date.*)

4. If the entry involves more than one page, cross-reference the pages.

5. If a mistake has been made, draw a line through the entry, initial and date it.

6. Draw a line through unused pages or blank spaces.

7. Have each notebook page signed and dated by a witness who has read and understands the entry.

8. Entries should be in chronological order.

9. If the experiment or reduction to practice has been witnessed, this fact should be recorded and signed by the witness.

10. The witness should not be a coinventor.

11. If the work was done under the supervision of another, this fact should be recorded.

12. Include references to other records such as analytical records, shipping and receiving receipts, and reports.

13. Do not make additions to pages that have been signed and dated.

14. Entries should describe the work done in sufficient clarity and detail as to enable someone of ordinary skill in the subject to repeat the work.

15. Do not state or suggest that the work has been or will be abandoned.

16. Other significant loose records (photographs, charts, etc.) should be permanently secured to blank pages of the notebook.

5

Researching
Your Ideas

Once you have documented conception, the next step is to research your idea to determine whether it is already in the public domain.

Searching the Literature

Conducting a literature search at the time of conception serves as a form of protection. Many people have wasted their time and money prototyping an invention only to discover afterward that someone else already did it. If they searched the literature first, perhaps they would have been able to protect their investment of time and money in the project. Depending on the costs associated with the project and its market potential, it may be worth while to have a patent practitioner assist with the search. The practitioner will not only assist in sifting through the information, but may make recomendations as to what course of action should be taken to design around any references that might otherwise render the invention as unpatentable. Thus, a good literature search, done at the time of conception, is a wise use of time and money and may result in better patent protection. There are several ways to search the technical and patent literature:

(1) Internet;

(2) online services;

(3) libraries;

(4) public search room at the U.S.P.T.O.; and

(5) professional search firms.

Some of these vehicles only provide access to the U.S. patent literature, while others afford access to U.S., foreign, and technical literature. The search should not be limited to only U.S. patents because all forms of references or prior art are taken into consideration when evaluating an invention for patentability. In addition, since everyone searches differently, it is beneficial to conduct a search using different resources and/or people.

> *TIP:* Search both the technical and patent literature before reducing your invention to practice.

INTERNET SEARCHING

The Internet is an excellent place to begin a search. Many researchers are making their work available on the Internet by posting articles on bulletin boards or on a website. In addition, many websites offer patent searching. Table 5.1 lists a few of the patent search

TABLE 5.1

Internet Search Sites

Site name	Website address	Features
U.S.P.T.O. Website	http://www.uspto.gov	Simple and advanced U.S. patent searching based on front page information from 1976 to present.
Chemical Patents Plus: From CAS	http://casweb.cas.org/chempatplus	Full text searching for all U.S. patents issued from1975 to present. Patent images for patents issued since 1994.
IBM Search Site	http://patent.womplex.ibm.com/	Patent searching from 1971 to present with images from 1975 to present.
MicroPatent	http://www.micropatent.com	U.S. patent searching from 1964 to present; European patent searching from 1978 to present; PCT applications from 1978 to present.
Shadow Patent Office	http://www.spo.eds.com/patent.html	Browse recently issued patents, guide to index and classification, perform a subject search. Full text U.S. patents from 1972 to present.
STO's Internet Patent Search System	http://sunsite.unc.edu/patents/intropat.html	Perform patent searches using the U.S.P.T.O. classification system.

sites available on the Internet. Most of these sites make it possible to order copies of patents directly from the site once the search is completed. Note that the search may not remain confidential and most of the databases only extend back to the 1970s. In addition, foreign patents are typically not included in the database.

COMMERCIAL ONLINE SERVICES

Commercial online services such as DIALOG, STN from Chem Abstracts, NERAC, and LEXIS are useful for searching both the technical and the patent literature. Having an account with one of these organizations permits access to a wide range of databases such as DERWENT's World Patent Index, and Biosis Embase. These are good search vehicles for newer technologies such as fiber optics and biotechnology. However, for older technologies these databases are not as useful because many of them only date back to the 1960s or 1970s. In addition, the results of these searches are only as good as the keywords provided. Therefore, it is best to combine this search vehicle with another.

LIBRARIES

After searching on the Internet or with an online service, go to the library. Having access to a technical library or an academic library is useful for searching nonpatent literature and possibly foreign references. A Patent and Trademark Depository Library (PTDL) is a good place to search the U.S. patent literature. Various PTDLs are located throughout the U.S. These libraries receive current issues of U.S. patents and maintain collections of earlier issued patents. Some of the libraries have all or most of the patents that issued dating from 1790. The PTDL is open to the public and the staff is excellent at assisting beginners with searching. A listing of the PTDLs is found in Appendix II.

PUBLIC SEARCH ROOM
AT THE U.S.P.T.O.

The U.S.P.T.O. has a public search room that makes all the U.S. patents granted since 1790 available. The patents are arranged according to the U.S. classification system where there are more than 400 classes and more than 136,000 subclasses. The patents are kept in "shoes" or small stacks on a shelf. Searching through the "shoes" is a manual search process. The searcher must actually look at every patent in the shoe. This can be time consuming but is usually more thorough than a keyword search. Another advantage to searching at the U.S.P.T.O. is that the Examiners are available to make suggestions as to where to search for the invention.

One disadvantage to searching at the U.S.P.T.O. is that from time to time the U.S.P.T.O. reclassifies the patents, removing entire classes or subclasses from the search room. If this occurs, the searcher will need to go to the examining group and conduct the search there. An advantage to searching within the examining group is that often the group's files contain foreign patents in addition to journal articles and the U.S. patents.

PROFESSIONAL SEARCH FIRMS

A number of professional search firms and services are available to assist in searching the literature as well as U.S. and foreign patents. To determine whether or not there is a local professional search firm in your area, look in the yellow pages under "patent searchers." If there are no search firms in your local area, go to your local library and consult the yellow pages for Washington, DC, Northern Virginia, Baltimore, or any major metropolitan city. Using a professional search firm is particularly useful for locating technical articles; some search firms specialize in certain technologies such as computer software or biotechnology.

Conducting a Search

Searching using electronic databases is fairly simple. Keywords relevant to the invention are entered into a database and the results are quickly generated. A disadvantage to this type of search is that the keywords used by some are not necessarily the same as those used by others. In particular, inventors who are new to the field and unfamiliar with the terminology often have trouble identifying keywords that will yield results.

Electronic databases are good search vehicles for those technologies which are new, such as fiber optics, and narrowly defined such as chemical compositions of matter. However, if the invention is for a mechanical device, the electronic database may not be as reliable unless drawings are provided. Many electronic databases only go back to the early 1970s. Thus, if one is conducting a search on an older technology, the electronic database may not produce reliable results.

When searching at the PTDLs or at the U.S.P.T.O., the following three publications need to be consulted before beginning the search:

(1) Index to classification

(2) Manual of classification

(3) Definitions of the classes and subclasses.

Most of this information is now contained on CD-ROM. When beginning the search, the index is consulted first. The index contains headings that are arranged alphabetically and cites the classes and subclass or group of subclasses for each subject. Once the class and subclass are identified for the invention, turn to the manual of classification. The manual lists every class and subclass numerically along with the title of the class or subclass. Consulting the manual may lead to subclasses that may be closer to the invention than those identified in the index. Lastly, the definitions further identify the subject matter assigned to each subclass and possible cross-references to related classes. After identifying the classes and subclasses, the patent bundles relating to the subclasses are obtained and the patents in the bundles reviewed for relevance.

When a relevant patent reference has been found, the information on the front of the patent may lead to more references. Figure 5.1 shows the front page of a patent. Note that some of the sections have field identifiers (the small numbers in brackets) and some of them do not. These field identifiers are used by the U.S.P.T.O. for data entry. Table 5.2 provides a brief explanation for each field identifier.

From a search perspective, the most important sections on the front of the patent are those relating to the references cited, U.S. classification, and field of search. Once a patent is identified that is close to the invention, the next step is to look at the references cited in the patent. These references were cited by the Examiner because they were considered to be material to the patentability of the invention described in the patent. It is likely that they may be relevant to the invention for which the search is being conducted and should be considered.

TIP: If a patent is identified that is close to the subject matter of the searched invention, look up the references cited on the front of the patent.

The references cited will also identify the classes and subclasses for the patents listed. The U.S. classification and field of search sections identify other classes and subclasses for the patented technology. As with the references cited, these other classes and subclasses should also be searched.

United States Patent [19]

Sandusky Donald A.

[11] **Patent Number:** **5,395,477**

[45] **Date of Patent:** **Mar. 7, 1995**

US005395477A

[54] **APPARATUS FOR CONSOLIDATING A PRE-IMPREGNATED, FILAMENT-REINFORCED POLYMERIC PREPREG MATERIAL**

[75] Inventor: Sandusky Donald A., Williamsburg, Va.

[73] Assignee: The United States of America as represented by the Administrator of the National Aeronautics and Space Administration, Washington, D.C.

[21] Appl. No.: 141,292

[22] Filed: Oct. 20, 1993

[51] Int. Cl.⁶ B29B 11/16; B29B 15/14; B29K 105/08

[52] U.S. Cl. 156/441; 156/180; 156/181; 156/433; 118/124; 264/136; 264/174

[58] Field of Search 156/180, 181, 166, 433, 156/441; 264/136, 174; 425/112, 114; 118/124

[56] **References Cited**

U.S. PATENT DOCUMENTS

2,407,335	9/1946	Wickwire, Jr.	118/124
3,249,484	5/1966	Courtney	156/181 X
3,737,352	6/1973	Avis et al.	156/181
3,993,726	11/1976	Moyer	264/174
4,549,920	10/1985	Cogswell et al.	156/181
4,610,402	9/1986	Corbett et al.	156/425 X
4,626,306	12/1986	Chabner et al.	156/180
4,804,509	2/1989	Angell et al.	264/136
4,919,739	4/1990	Dyksterhouse et al.	156/181

5,094,883	3/1992	Muzzy et al.	427/434.6 X
5,296,064	3/1994	Muzzy et al.	156/180

FOREIGN PATENT DOCUMENTS

550432	3/1993	Japan	156/180
1434926	5/1976	United Kingdom	118/124
422469	9/1974	U.S.S.R.	118/124

Primary Examiner—Jeff H. Aftergut
Attorney, Agent, or Firm—George F. Helfrich; Joy L. Bryant

[57] **ABSTRACT**

An apparatus and method were developed for providing a uniform, consolidated, unidirectional, continuous, fiber-reinforced polymeric material. The apparatus comprises a supply means, a forming means, a shaping means, and a take-up means. The forming means further comprises a pre-melting chamber and a stationary bar assembly. The shaping means is a loaded cooled nip-roller apparatus. Forming takes place by heating a polymeric prepreg material to a temperature where the polymer becomes viscous and applying pressure gradients at separate locations along the prepreg material. Upon exiting the forming means, the polymeric prepreg material is malleable, consolidated and flattened. Shaping takes place by passing the malleable, consolidated, flattened prepreg material through a shaped, matched groove in a loaded, cooled nip-roller apparatus to provide the final solid product.

6 Claims, 5 Drawing Sheets

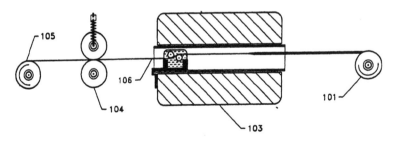

FIGURE 5.1

Front page of a utility patent. The numbers in brackets are field identifiers.

TABLE 5.2

Field Identifiers for U.S. Patents

Field Number	Designation
11	U.S. patent number
19	U.S. patent and first-named inventor's last name
21	Patent application serial number
22	Date the patent application was filed (note patent term calculated based on this date for patents filed after June 8, 1995)
45	Date the patent issued
51	International patent classification number
52	U.S. patent classification numbers, the first being the class and the second the subclass
54	Title of the invention
56	References cited by the Examiner and the applicant indicating the state-of-the-art for the invention
57	An abstract describing the invention
58	Classes and subclasses searched by the Examiner to determine patentability of the invention
73	Company, organization, or individual who owns the patent
75	Inventor's full name

TIP: Do not forget to search the classes and subclasses identified in the sections relating to the field of search and U.S. classification.

Sometimes an inventor's name can be a useful search tool, especially if that inventor is known to have patents for a particular technology. This is typical for patents assigned to corporations, institutions of higher education, and federal laboratories where the projects are ongoing. Conducting a search on an inventor's name will reveal all of the patents for that particular individual.

TIP: If you know the name of an inventor who has worked on a particular technology, conducting a search on his or her name may be helpful.

Another item to search is the name of a particular assignee (or company name). If the subject technology of the search is currently manufactured by a particular company, searching the assignee's name will reveal patents (if any) that may be relevant. For example, suppose the invention is for a shoe, searching on Nike as the assignee will result in a listing of all the patents owned by Nike.

TIP: Company names are useful to include in a search.

A Brief Word about Prototyping the Invention

Once the literature search has been completed, the inventor should have a good idea of how others have attempted to solve the problem. Alternative solutions described in the references are useful for designing and prototyping an invention. If a reference is found that is on-point with the original invention, ways to design around that which was disclosed should be considered. The design and fabrication of the invention should be recorded in the laboratory notebook in such a way that someone else working on the same problem can reproduce the work. Ideally, making the invention using the same materials that a manufacturer will use to make the final product is best. However, if funds are limited or the materials are not readily available, the invention may be prototyped using low-cost substitutions. Prototyping the invention leads to proof that the concept works. In addition, prototyping establishes the best way to carry out the invention.

All work on the invention should be recorded in the lab notebook, including failures. Recording experimental failures and successes serves many uses during patent prosecution. For example, during prosecution providing a showing of what did not work helps to more clearly define the invention.

Lastly, if a prototype cannot be constructed, one may file a provisional or a regular patent application in the U.S.P.T.O. setting forth the details of the invention. This will serve as a constructive reduction to practice as of its filing date.

TIP: There are two ways to reduce the invention to practice:

(1) build a prototype; or

(2) file a patent application in the U.S.P.T.O.

Review

Before beginning work on an invention, conduct a search to determine whether it is already in the public domain. Both the technical and patent literature should be searched using several different vehicles. When the patent literature is searched and a relevant patent found, information on the front of the patent may be used to identify other relevant patents. The search results should be used to assess the invention and to move forward with production of a prototype.

6

Protect Yourself

Certain events may prohibit or jeopardize your patent rights. This chapter focuses on what you need to do to protect yourself from forfeiting your right to patent in the U.S. and in foreign countries.

Avoid Statutory Bars

Many inventors are very excited once they have successfully reduced their invention to practice. In jubilation, some will immediately start to show, tell, and sell their inventions before they have filed their patent application. Unfortunately, all these acts impact one's right to obtain a patent. These acts and others are defined in title 35 of the United States Code (35 U.S.C.) and are called *statutory bars*.

Most foreign countries require that a patent application must be filed before the invention is publicly disclosed; otherwise, the invention is not patentable. This type of requirement is called an *absolute novelty* requirement. The U.S. does not have this type of requirement. Instead, the U.S. grants a 1-year grace period from the time the invention is first made public, either by the inventor or by someone else, in which one may file a patent application for that invention.

The acts which may eliminate one's opportunity to obtain a patent or that start the 1-year grace period are set forth in 35 U.S.C. §102. This section of the code defines novelty. All of these acts are date-sensitive and may be committed by:

(1) others,

(2) the inventor, or

(3) both the inventor and others.

ACTS BY OTHERS

Certain acts occurring before the date of invention will prevent a person from being awarded a patent for the invention. These acts include knowledge or use of the invention in the U.S.,[1] patenting or describing the invention in a printed publication anywhere in the world.[2]

It is important to realize that known or used differs from patented or published. By known or used, it is meant that the information must be accessible to the public and that one can prove its existence. The issue is one of public knowledge. For example, if it is public knowledge that ethanol may be safely consumed as a beverage by human beings, then one may not obtain a patent for the use of ethanol to make beverages for human consumption.

Patent rights are lost if before the applicant's date of invention, the invention is patented or described in a printed publication anywhere in the world. The applicant does not have to be aware of the publication. Therefore, references published in foreign countries may be used as references to prevent a person from getting a patent for an invention. Publications are not limited to patents and technical articles. For example, trade catalogs are treated as publications[3] as well as theses and dissertations[4] if they have been catalogued and are available to the public in a library. In addition, abstracts of talks presented at technical meetings are also considered to be publications if they are made publicly available. Although not yet litigated, it is safe to assume that articles published on the Internet are also considered to be publications.

EXAMPLE

A new polymer made from monomers A and B was invented. A Japanese abstract, published before the date of the invention and disclosing a polymer produced from monomers A and B, was found during a literature search. Because of the teaching in the abstract, the inventor was barred from getting a patent.

WARNING: Publication of the invention before the applicant's date of invention will prevent the applicant from obtaining a patent for the invention.

WARNING: The applicant does not have to be aware of the reference that discloses the invention.

TIP: If time and resources permit, conduct both a U.S. and a foreign literature search in addition to an Internet search before filing for a patent.

Another act that may be committed by others that will prevent a person from obtaining a patent relates to what others disclose in their patents. If another patent describes the invention but does not claim it, before the date of the applicant's invention, then no patent will be granted to the applicant.[5] The interesting fact about this type of bar is that some patents serve as *secret prior art.*

Secret prior art results because the reference date of the patent is its filing date. Therefore, it is possible to have a patent that issues after an applicant's filing date, cited against the applicant because it has a filing date earlier than the applicant's filing date.

Secret prior art references are often overcome by submitting an affidavit showing that the date of invention was prior to the filing date of the issued patent. However, for the nonsecret prior art, arguments must be presented to try to show that the applicant's invention differs from that disclosed in the patent. If no such argument may be made, then no patent will be awarded.

Lastly, if before the applicant's date of invention, another party makes the invention and does not abandon, suppress, or conceal it, a patent will not be awarded to the applicant.[6] For example, if there are two pending patent applications or a pending patent application and a patent that issued within 1-year that claim the same invention, an interference is declared within the U.S.P.T.O. As noted earlier, the patent is awarded to the party who can prove priority of invention.

ACTS BY THE INVENTOR

The inventor may cause certain events to occur before he or she files a patent application that will jeopardize his or her right to patent. Such events include abandoning the invention,[7] not being the original inventor,[8] or filing and patenting the invention in a foreign country more than 12 months before filing in the U.S.[9]

Abandonment occurs when the inventor commits any one of the following acts:

(1) completely stops working on the invention;

(2) secretly uses the invention and later decides to file a patent application upon discovery that another is using the invention;

(3) publicly renounces his or her intention to apply for a patent; or

(4) discontinues prosecution of a pending patent application for the invention.

One way an inventor publicly renounces intention to apply for a patent is by writing statements such as "this invention has been abandoned" in the laboratory notebook. This practice should be avoided.

> *TIP:* Do not write or suggest that your invention will be abandoned.

Note that one cannot choose to protect an invention by trade secret, publicly sell the invention, and later opt to file a patent application for the invention. Such activity is construed as a forfeiture of patent rights.

EXAMPLE

In *Macbeth-Evans Glass Co. v. General Electric Co.*,[10] the court found that the decision to keep an invention a trade secret instead of filing a patent application constituted abandonment. In this case, Macbeth discovered and perfected the formula and process for making glass for illuminating purposes in the fall of 1903. The company, Macbeth-Evans Glass Co. decided to keep the formula and the process as a trade secret, selling the resulting products to the public. In May 1910, one of the company's employees left the company and disclosed the trade secrets to Jefferson Glass Company, who proceeded to secretly use the invention. In May 1913, a patent application was filed by Macbeth. At this time, Macbeth-Evans Glass Co. filed suit against the former employee and Jefferson Glass Company. The court enjoined the former employee and Jefferson Glass Company from making any glass protected by the secret process. However, the patent was found to be invalid under abandonment because Macbeth had originally decided not to pursue patent protection until the theft of the trade secret had occurred. Note that this is a very old case and under today's laws, the invention would not be patentable because of its public use (discussed later in this chapter).

A person is not the original inventor if the invention is derived from someone else. Derivation occurs when someone sees someone else's invention and decides to file a patent application for the invention in his or her own name. Typically, issues of derivation are discovered during litigation.

EXAMPLE

When the first multipurpose, programmable digital computers were invented, two researchers at the University of Pennsylvania filed a patent for the technology. During a patent suit, it was discovered that the two inventors had actually derived their ideas from a professor at Iowa State University.[11] The patent was found to be invalid.

—————

Filing a patent application in a foreign country more than 1 year before filing in the U.S. and having the patent issue in a foreign country before filing in the U.S. will result in a loss of one's right to patent in the U.S. All of the following conditions must be met to lose one's right to patent in the U.S.:

(1) the invention must be the same invention that one is applying for a patent on in the U.S.;

(2) the foreign patent must issue before the U.S. patent application is filed; and

(3) the U.S. patent application must be filed more than 12 months after the foreign patent application was filed.

EXAMPLES

(A) Hans files a patent application in Germany on February 9, 1996. On December 9, 1996, he files a similar patent application in the U.S. On January 2, 1997, Hans' German-filed patent application issues. Hans is not prevented from getting a patent in the U.S. because his U.S. application was filed within 12 months of his German application and before the German patent issued (Fig. 6.1A).

(B) Hans files a patent application in Germany on February 9, 1996. On December 9, 1996, his German-filed patent application issues. On February 8, 1997, Hans files a patent application in the U.S. Hans is not prevented from getting a patent because his U.S. application filing date is within 1 year of filing his German application (Fig. 6.1B).

(C) Hans files a patent application in Germany on February 9, 1996. On June 9, 1997, Hans files his U.S. patent application. On August 10, 1997, Hans' German-filed patent application issues. Hans is not precluded from getting a U.S. patent because his German filed application did not issue before he filed in the U.S. However, Hans will lose the benefit of his German filing date in accordance with the Paris Convention because he did not file within one year of his German application (Fig. 6.1C).

TIP: To avoid losing the right to patent, follow one basic rule of thumb: file a patent application in the U.S. within 1 year of filing an application anywhere else.

ACTS BY THE INVENTOR AND/OR OTHERS

Lastly, an inventor can be prohibited from obtaining a patent because of acts committed more than 1 year before filing in the U.S. These acts include patenting the invention, publishing the invention, using the invention in public, and/or selling the invention. Patenting or publishing the invention is the most common statutory bar. Many inventors publish articles about their inventions before they file a

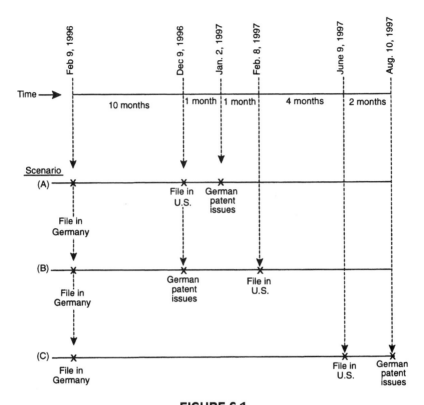

FIGURE 6.1

U.S. filings based on a foreign-originated patent application. (A) Hans files his U.S. application within 10 months of his German application. (B) Hans' German patent issues before he files in the U.S. but the U.S. application is filed within 1 year of the German application date. (C) Hans files in the U.S. more than 1 year after filing in Germany but prior to his German patent issuing.

patent application. This activity starts the "1-year clock" whereby the inventor must file a patent application within 1 year of the publication date in order to preserve the right to patent. Note that a patent or printed publication is similar to that explained in the section "Acts by Others." However, in this instance, the patent or printed

publication may be authored by the inventor and occur
date of invention, where before, the patent or printed ｐ
had to be authored by others and publication had to occur
date of invention.

EXAMPLES

(A) Ruth invented a new needle to be used for
counted cross-stitch on February 10, 1996. On
August 14, 1996, she published an article in a
trade magazine disclosing the new needle. On
August 15, 1997, she filed a patent application.
Ruth was barred from getting a patent for her
new needle because she filed her application
more than 1 year after the publication date of
the trade magazine.

(B) Ed invented a new calculator on July 4, 1996. On
August 4, 1996, Andy authored and published an
article about the new calculator in a computer
journal. On August 3, 1997, Ed filed a patent application claiming the new calculator. Ed was not
precluded from getting a patent because he
filed within 1 year of the publication date of
Andy's journal article (Fig. 6.2).

An interesting contrast between the U.S. patent system and the
systems of many foreign countries is that most foreign countries do
not have a 1-year grace period in which to file. Instead, the application must be filed before any publication of the invention occurs.

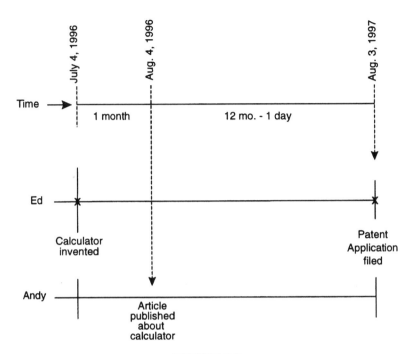

FIGURE 6.2

Time line showing how Andy's publication serves as a statutory bar for Ed as of the August 4, 1996 publication date.

> *TIP:* If you are planning on protecting your invention in a foreign country, file your patent application before you make your invention public.

Another act that may prevent a person from obtaining a patent is public use of the invention more than 1 year prior to the filing date of the patent application.

Public use of an invention occurs when an inventor gives or sells the invention to another person to use without putting any limitations or restrictions on that use.

The key to avoiding the issue of public use is that the inventor must retain control over the use of the invention as well as controlling the distribution and information concerning it. For example, it was found that a kaleidoscope[12] placed on display and demonstrated at a party attended by 20–30 guests, constituted a public use of the invention. The inventor never made an effort to conceal the device or keep anything about it secret. This was in contrast to another case[13] where the inventor had displayed his device to his friends and it was found that there was an implied restriction of confidentiality, thus not constituting a public use. An exception to public use is an experimental use of the invention.[14]

Experimental use is a use of an invention by the inventor or by another person under the inventor's direction, by way of experiment, in order to perfect the invention.

The key to experimental use is that the inventor engages, in good faith, in testing the operation of the invention. As with public use, the inventor must not let the invention go beyond his control. However, if the inventor decides to profit from selling or using the invention, then the experimental use exception does not apply.

Lastly, if an invention is sold or offered for sale, it triggers an on-sale bar or the 1-year time in which a regular patent application must be filed. A sale includes an offer for sale, whether the offer is accepted or not. Three tests are applied in determining whether a sale of the invention has occurred[15,16]:

(1) the complete invention must be embodied in or obvious in view of the thing offered for sale;

(2) the invention must have been tested to verify that it is operable and commercially marketable; and

(3) the sale must be for profit rather than experimental purposes.

Note that although one of the tests specifies operability, the invention does not have to be reduced to practice for an offer of sale to occur.[17] Instead, one must consider the circumstances surrounding the sale, the stage of development of the invention, and the nature of the invention. For example, if the inventor had only a concept or was working toward developing a concept, there is no sale. However, if the concept has been worked out and the offer for sale is to work toward commercializing the invention, it is a bar. Such was the case with UMC Electronics who offered their invention for sale by bidding on a government contract.[18] Although the invention claimed in their patent was not reduced to practice at the time they submitted their bid, their intention was to profit from the sale of the invention. The court found that the invention was on-sale for more than 1 year before they filed their patent application and the patent was declared invalid.

Many people confuse an offer for sale with publication of the invention. This usually occurs when the invention is offered for sale in a proposal. Although many proposals are kept confidential and are not available to the public, if the intention of the proposal is to work toward commercializing the invention, then the on-sale bar applies despite the fact that the publication bar does not apply.

> *WARNING:* If you are submitting your invention in a proposal with the intention of profiting from it, you are triggering an on-sale bar.

Several policies underlying the on-sale bar must be considered when determining whether the on-sale bar applies.[19]

(1) There is a policy against removing inventions from the public when the public believes the inventions were freely available because of prolonged sales activity.

(2) A policy exists that favors prompt and widespread disclosure of new inventions to the public by promptly filing a patent application.

(3) Third, a policy exists that prevents the inventor from commercially exploiting the exclusivity of the invention beyond the term of the patent.

(4) Lastly, a policy exists that gives the inventor a reasonable amount of time (1 year) to file a patent application after the first sales activity of the invention.

If any of these policies are violated, the on-sale bar applies. An application must be filed within 1 year of the first sale or offer to sell in order to obtain a patent for the invention. Note that a sale of a product or process made in accordance with a patent differs from *licensing* or *assigning* a patent. In a sale, the product is made according to the invention. The subject of a license or an assignment is the invention itself, not the product. Therefore, licensing or assigning a patent or patent application does not constitute a sale of the invention.

Review

It is important to be aware of statutory bars and how they are triggered. If a statutory bar is triggered, most likely the inventor has put his or her foreign patent rights into jeopardy and has started the 1-year grace period in the U.S. Table 6.1 summarizes the statutory bars.

TABLE 6.1

Summary of Statutory Bars

Acts preventing one from obtaining a patent	Acts starting the 1-year clock
Abandoning the invention or a pending patent application	Describing the invention in a printed publication in the U.S. or a foreign country
Public knowledge or use of the invention *before* the date of invention	Offering the invention for sale, including offers made under a confidential agreement
Invention already patented in the U.S. or a foreign country *before* the date of invention	Public, nonexperimental, use of the invention
Invention described in a printed publication *before* the date of invention	Filing a patent application in a foreign country
Invention described in another person's patent *before* the date of invention	
Invention was already made by another who had not abandoned, suppressed, or concealed it *before* the applicant's invention	
Invention patented more than one year before *filing* a patent application	
Person seeking a patent is *not* the true inventor	

Annotated References

1. 35 U.S.C. §102(a). *(Statute relating to public knowledge or use before date of the invention.)*
2. 35 U.S.C. §102(a). *(Statute relating to patented or printed in a publication before the date of invention.)*

3. Jockmus v. Leviton, 28 F.2d 812 (2d Cir. 1928). *(Precedent for trade catalogs serving as printed publications.)*

4. In re Hall, 781 F.2d 897, 228 U.S.P.Q. (BNA) 453 (Fed. Cir. 1986).

5. 35 U.S.C. §102(e). *(Statute relating to the invention being described in a patent granted to another before the applicant's date of invention.)*

6. 35 U.S.C. §102(g). *(Statute relating to invention by another who had not abandoned, suppressed, or concealed the invention.)*

7. 35 U.S.C. §102(c). *(Statute relating to inventor abandoning the invention.)*

8. 35 U.S.C. §102(f). *(Statute relating to a person not being the original inventor.)*

9. 35 U.S.C. §102(d). *(Statute relating to foreign filing and patenting before the U.S. filing date.)*

10. Macbeth-Evans Glass Co. v. General Electric Co., 246 F. 695 (6th Cir. 1917). *(Precedent for abandonment.)*

11. Iowa State University Research Foundation v. Sperry Rand Corporation, 444 F. 2d 406, 170 U.S.P.Q. 374 (4th Cir. 1971). *(Case showing derivation of an invention.)*

12. Beachcombers, International, Inc. and Patrick MacCarthy v. Wildewood Creative Products, Inc., 31 F.3d 1154 (1994); 31 U.S.P.Q. 2D (BNA) 1653. *(Case showing public use.)*

13. Moleculon Research Corp. v. CBS, Inc., 793 F.2d 1261, 229 U.S.P.Q. (BNA) 805. *(Case showing public use.)*

14. City of Elizabeth v. American Nicholson Pavement Co., 97 U.S. 126 (1877). *(Precedent for experimental use.)*

15. In re Corcoran, 640 F. 2d 1331, 1333-34, 208 U.S.P.Q. 867, 870 (C.C.P.A. 1981). *(Precedent for the three part test for on-sale bar.)*

16. Timely Prods. Corp. v. Arron, 523 F.2d 288, 302, 187 U.S.P.Q. 257, 267-68 (2d Cir. 1975). *(Precedent for the three part test for on-sale bar.)*

17. UMC Electronics Co. v. United States, 816 F.2d 647, 2 U.S.P.Q.2d (BNA) 1465 (Fed. Cir. 1987). *(Precedent for reduction to practice not necessary for an offer for sale to occur.)*

18. Ibid.

19. General Electric Co. v. United States, 654 F.2d 55, 60-61, 211 U.S.P.Q. 867, 872-73 (Ct. Cl. 1981) (en banc). *(Policies with respect to the on-sale bar.)*

7

Preparing the
Patent Application

The patent process is a complex legal process. This chapter gives an overview of how to prepare for the patent process and some insight as to why you need a patent practitioner to help you with the process.

Representing Yourself

Inventors have the right to represent themselves in the U.S. Patent and Trademark Office (U.S.P.T.O.). The question is, do they want to? The patent process is a legal process. It is similar in complexity to preparing and filing a 1040 income tax return for a small business. Many people prepare and file their own income tax returns. However, after doing so, some may wonder if they would have saved more money if they had a professional prepare their return for them. A similar level of uncertainty is found among those who attempt to prepare their own patent applications. Obtaining the best patent protection for an invention and navigating through the patent system requires a continuous study of the patent laws and regulations. If a person is willing to invest several years of his or her life studying patent law, chances are the patents prepared by that person will provide the protection needed. However, most inventors do not want to concern themselves studying patent law.

Having proper representation in the U.S.P.T.O. affords certain benefits. For example, the practitioner has experience working with the Examiners and the support staff at the U.S.P.T.O. and knows what to expect. Occasionally, unexpected events occur during the patent process. The typical "how to" books do not address how to resolve the issues associated with these events. Therefore, it is difficult for someone who is unfamiliar with the patent system to detect what is normal and what is not. The following examples reflect on two unexpected events that occurred in the author's patent practice.

EXAMPLES

(1) A provisional patent application was filed. When the return postal card was received, it was noted that the U.S.P.T.O. assigned a series number to the provisional application that they typically assign to a regular application. Proper action had to be taken to correct this. Most self-help books do not notify the readers that the U.S.P.T.O. assigns different series numbers to different types of patent applications. If they do, there is no instruction how to correct such a mistake. How-

ever, the patent practitioner is alert to these types of mistakes and knows how to handle them.

(2) In another incident, a notice was received that the Examiner allowed a patent application. Attached to the notice was an Examiner Interview Summary that summarized a conversation between the applicant's practitioner and the Examiner. When the practitioner reviewed the summary, she discovered that the information recorded by the Examiner contradicted the allowed claims. This type of mistake must be corrected in case the patent is ever litigated.

Patent Practitioners

A **patent practitioner** is a person who is registered to practice patent law before the U.S. Patent and Trademark Office.

Not all intellectual property attorneys can represent clients in the U.S.P.T.O. Those people representing clients before the U.S.P.T.O. must pass the *patent bar* exam. The patent bar exam is a special examination administered once per year by the U.S.P.T.O. Office of Enrollment and Discipline. The exam tests the candidate's knowledge of the patent laws, regulations, and procedure within the U.S.P.T.O. To take the exam, the candidate must have, at a minimum, enough credit hours in a specific discipline, as specified by the U.S.P.T.O.,[1] or a Bachelor's degree in a recognized technical field such as biology, chemistry, physics, or engineering. Many lawyers do not meet this requirement. Thus, the U.S.P.T.O. allows individuals who meet the requirements to take the same patent bar examination as the attorneys who meet the requirements. The U.S.P.T.O. registers the nonlawyers who pass the examination to practice patent law within the U.S.P.T.O. as *patent agents.* The lawyers who pass the examination are registered to practice as *patent attorneys.*

> **Patent agents** are nonlawyers who have passed the patent bar examination and are registered to practice patent law before the U.S.P.T.O.

> **Patent attorneys** are lawyers who have passed a state bar examination and the patent bar examination and are registered to practice patent law before the U.S.P.T.O. in addition to representing a client in a court of law.

> *WARNING:* Not all intellectual property attorneys are patent practitioners.

> *TIP:* Ask your intellectual property attorney if he or she is registered to practice before the U.S.P.T.O.

> *TIP:* Call the Office of Enrollment and Discipline (see Appendix I) to find out if someone is registered to practice before the U.S.P.T.O.

Patent attorneys can practice all aspects of patent law. Not only can they help an individual get a patent but they may also:

- prepare assignments;
- negotiate and prepare licensing agreements;
- render infringement opinions;
- give market clearances; and
- litigate the patent.

Patent agents are specialists. They focus on preparing and prosecuting patent applications. Patent agents are helpful because they:

- specialize in procedure before the U.S.P.T.O.;
- focus on preparing and prosecuting patent applications; and
- typically have advanced technical degrees or industrial experience.

WATCH OUT FOR
INVENTION DEVELOPERS

Many inventors have been ripped-off by unscrupulous invention development firms. Some advertise on late night television, in the classified sections of magazines, and more recently on the Internet. They typically offer the inventor a supposedly low-cost way of getting a patent and marketing the invention. They will claim to represent manufacturers who are looking for new ideas. Some will offer a contract where they agree to help an inventor market and license the invention. This contract usually has a large price tag ($5,000–$10,000) associated with it. Reputable licensing firms usually do not require large advance fees from the inventor.

> *TIP:* If an invention developer claims to have a relationship with a certain manufacturer, ask for proof before signing a contract with them.

Some invention developers charge high fees to file a Disclosure Document in the U.S.P.T.O. An inventor can do this him or herself for $10. Other firms have filed the wrong type of patent application or they have filed no patent application at all and have charged the client an unreasonably high fee to do so. Many inventors get conned by these firms each year. Appendix III provides some helpful information with respect to invention development firms.

TIP: Try to avoid using an invention development firm.

SELECTING A PATENT PRACTITIONER

Most academic inventors and corporate inventors do not need to concern themselves with finding and selecting a patent practitioner. In these environments, the patent practitioner is usually preselected. However, for the individual inventor, finding and selecting a patent practitioner is a new process and there are several ways to do so:

(1) Look in the yellow pages section of the telephone book under "patent agents" and "patent attorneys."

(2) Search the roster of attorneys and agents by accessing the U.S.P.T.O.'s website (information in Appendix I).

(3) Get a referral from someone who has been through the patent process.

(4) Contact the National Association of Patent Practitioners.

Looking in the yellow pages or searching the roster are ways of locating a practitioner in a particular geographic location. However, geography is not an issue with today's telecommunication capabilities. Obtaining a referral from someone who, in the past, has used a particular patent practitioner affords the advantage of knowing about the practitioner's reputation before entering into the patent process with him or her. Lastly, the National Association of Patent Practitioners maintains a roster of attorneys and agents who are members of the organization. This roster identifies practitioner members by their geographic location and by their areas of scientific expertise. This is particularly helpful if the invention is in a specialized field.

Once a practitioner has been found, conduct an interview and find out about the practitioner's background. Patent practice is specialized based on the technology. For example, if the invention is for a new gene therapy, one may not want a patent practitioner with an electrical engineering background to work on the patent. By asking the practitioner about his or her background and experience one can easily determine whether the practitioner's background is a match with the technology of the invention. Feeling comfortable with the patent practitioner is important because all the details of the invention must be revealed to this person. If the inventor does not feel comfortable doing this, the patent process will be an uphill battle.

TIP: Interview several patent practitioners before selecting your representative.

Preparing for an Effective Practitioner Interview

Many inventors never meet a patent practitioner until they are ready to file a patent application. Every practitioner needs certain information to properly prepare the patent application. Having this information assembled before seeing a patent practitioner will maximize the efficiency of the first appointment and save money in preparing the application if there is an hourly rate charge.

A list of the names of all the people who worked on or who contributed to the invention is needed. This list should include the full names of the individuals, their home addresses and their countries of citizenship. The practitioner uses this information to determine the correct *inventorship* and prepare the *declaration.* If the invention has a title, that should also be provided along with a description of the technical area for the invention. This helps the practitioner categorize the invention for searching and rendering a *patentability* opinion. Inventions resulting from work that was federally funded or funded under some type of contractual agreement will require supplying the name of the agency and the grant number. The U.S. government has a royalty free license to any invention that results from a U.S. government contract and a statement showing this must be included in the patent application.

To find out if the inventor has started the 1-year grace period, the practitioner needs to know if and when any of the following events occurred:

(a) invention first displayed in public;

(b) invention described in a publication such as an abstract for a technical meeting, a scientific paper, press release, or placed on the Internet;

(c) invention described orally at a public meeting;

(d) inventor's intention to publish the invention within the next 6 months;

(e) invention offered for sale–remember that submitting a write-up of the invention in a proposal with the intention to commercialize the invention is an offer for sale;[2]

(f) invention revealed to a third party and if the inventor revealed it under a *confidentiality agreement*. Note that a confidentiality agreement is an agreement between two parties in which they agree that the subject information will be kept secret.

A written description of the problem to be solved and any relevant publications that discuss the problem are helpful in understanding the background of the invention. Identifying how others tried to solve the problem and their failures helps show the shortcomings of any prior inventions. A description showing how the invention solves the problems helps both the inventor and the practitioner identify the true invention. A drawing or drawings showing each physical or functional element (preferably numbered) of the invention is extremely helpful for understanding the invention. Once the drawing is complete and numbered, a written description referring to each numbered part shown in the drawing should describe how the parts interact with each other to solve the problems described earlier. The picture does not have to be computer-generated although most practitioners prefer it.

One should also describe different variations to the invention. This information helps the patent practitioner broaden the patent coverage for the invention instead of limiting the coverage to one specific device. If the inventor provides no variations, the practitioner may ask questions to help the inventor broaden the concept.

Describing the structural and/or functional differences between the invention and that which previously exists helps the practitioner distinguish the invention over the prior art. This distinction brings out the *novelty* of the invention. Listing reasons why the inventor believes his or her solution to the problem would not be apparent to others working on the same problem helps the practitioner identify the *nonobvious* features of the invention. For example, if the invention is the discovery that humans can safely consume ethanol, the individual would state, "Methanol and propanol are toxic when consumed by humans. My invention is for ethanol, which humans can safely consume."

If the inventor constructed a prototype of the invention, instructions describing how to make it should be provided. Provide enough detail in these instructions so someone else can reproduce the invention. If the invention has not been constructed, then instructions describing how the inventor thinks the invention could be made should be provided. The inventor should give examples of experiments that failed or experiments that did not work as well as the invention. This information may be used to make a showing of the best way to carry out the invention besides bringing out the nonobvious features of the invention.

A list of the possible uses for the invention shows *utility* and aids the practitioner in understanding the intended use for the invention. Usually, the uses are readily apparent.

Lastly, having a laboratory notebook and any other records for the invention available shows how the invention has been documented. The practitioner may need to rely on these documents at some point during the patent process.

After assembling this information, the inventor is ready to visit a patent practitioner. The information supplied will be used to evaluate the invention for patentability, prepare the patent application, and prepare the accompanying formal papers. Appendix IV lists the information the patent practitioner needs.

The Requirements for Patentability

Prior to preparing and filing a patent application, it is important to determine whether the invention is patentable based on the following three tests for patentability:

(1) utility[3]

(2) novelty[4]

(3) nonobviousness[5]

UTILITY

To meet the utility requirement, the invention must be able to accomplish three things:

(1) It must be operable.

(2) It must solve the problem it was designed to solve.

(3) It must provide a minimum benefit to society.

Most inventions meet the utility requirement. Rarely is a device invented without having a particular use in mind. However, inventions relating to new chemical compounds or genetic sequences sometimes have difficulty meeting the utility requirement. This usually occurs when a scientist is exploring a general class of compounds and a new compound is invented, but its use is not yet identified. Similarly, inventions relating to chemical processes may not always meet the utility requirement because it must be shown that the product from the process is useful for some specific purpose other than being an end product of the process. Sometimes, this cannot be achieved.

Some people make the mistake of thinking that an invention must be commercially successful to be useful. This is not true. The invention does not have to be commercially marketable or have outstanding performance characteristics to meet the utility requirement. However, the invention must benefit society in some way. If the invention is considered harmful to the public, then the utility requirement is not met. An example of an invention deemed harmful to the public in 1897 was a slot machine.[6] However, society's standards have since changed. Today, this type of invention would be patentable because it provides amusement.

NOVELTY

An invention is novel if every element of the invention is not:

- found in a single prior art reference;

- previously known; or
- part of a single prior art device or practice.

Prior art is the body of technical information that was available or accessible to the public at the time of or before the invention.

Usually prior to the preparation and filing of a patent application, a search of the prior art is conducted. An invention is not novel or is *anticipated* if there is an identity formed between a single prior art reference and the invention. Therefore, if a *single reference* shows or describes *every* feature of the invention, the invention lacks novelty and is not patentable. The following example reflects how the analysis for anticipation or novelty is conducted. Note that the analysis compares every element of the invention to the elements found in a single patent.

EXAMPLE

Jacob Whitlock[7] invented a railroad grade crossing cover laid over the railroad ties and between the rails. An overlapping splicer piece connects segments of the grade crossing cover to one another.

A patent, issued to Rennels, discloses a railroad crossing cover laid over railroad ties and between the rails. The crossing cover has a one-piece rubber center section reinforced with a corrugated metal plate that rests on top of the rubber laid between the tracks.

A comparison of the invention of Whitlock to the Rennels patent shows that the Rennels patent does not have each and every element of the Whitlock invention. Although both the Whitlock invention and the Rennels patent include a grade crossing cover laid over ties and between rails, the Rennels patent did not reveal the overlapping splicer piece. Therefore, the Rennels patent does not anticipate the Whitlock invention or, in other words, the Whitlock invention is novel.

NONOBVIOUSNESS

An invention is *nonobvious* if a person of ordinary skill in the art cannot readily deduce it from the prior art.

The differences between the invention and the prior art must be such that the subject matter as a whole would not have been obvious to a person having ordinary skill in the art. Nonobviousness is perhaps the most critical test for patentability and the most difficult test for an invention to pass. It is a subjective test based on the viewpoint of a person of ordinary skill in the art to which the invention relates. Who is this person? The one of ordinary skill in the art is a hypothetical person. To construct a reasonable profile of this person, the level of ordinary skill for the technology must be determined and applied to the hypothetical person. Several factors are taken into consideration when making this determination, such as:

(1) educational level of the inventor;

(2) type of problems encountered in the art;

(3) prior art solutions;

(4) speed at which innovations are being made;

(5) level of sophistication of the technology; and

(6) educational level of workers in the field.[8]

The test for nonobviousness is such that it prevents patents from issuing for inventions that offer only a trivial step forward for a technology. Typically, if a single reference does not anticipate an invention, the next step is for the U.S.P.T.O. to determine whether the invention would have been obvious to one of ordinary skill in the art. This is made by either combining several references and stating that the invention is obvious or by relying on a single reference in combination with the knowledge of one of ordinary skill in the art. The burden then shifts to the patent applicant to show that the invention is not obvious in view of the combination of references cited. The following example shows how the U.S.P.T.O. puts together an argument for obviousness.

EXAMPLE

A conductive polymer composition exhibiting improved physical properties and having a molecular weight which is greater than 150,000 was invented.[9] The composition was based on commercially available high-molecular-weight polymers having certain physical properties. The U.S.P.T.O. rejected the patent application claiming this invention was obvious. They asserted that selecting commercially available polymers of high-molecular-weight to obtain better physical properties would have been obvious for one of ordinary skill in the art.

When a patent practitioner is evaluating an invention for patentability, all information that was publicly available at the time of the invention is considered. If the invention passes the tests for utility, novelty, and nonobviousness, the invention is given a favorable patentability opinion and the next step is to prepare a patent application.

Preparing the Regular Utility Patent Application

A patent application is not like a job application. It is not a form, but it is a legal and a technical document. Every patent application has specific sections that must be completed. However, the written content that goes into these sections differs from one invention to the next or is invention specific. Regular utility patent applications contain:

(1) at least one *claim;*

(2) a *specification;*

(3) a *drawing* (if necessary); and

(4) an *abstract.*

CLAIMS

Most patent practitioners begin writing a patent application by drafting a set of claims directed toward the invention. Remember, the claims are the part of the patent that sets forth the definition of the technology that is exclusively owned by the patentee for the term of the patent. The practitioner drafts each claim as a single sentence taken with the introductory words, "I (We) claim," "What is claimed is," or other similar language. The length of the sentence is unspecified but each numbered claim must only be one sentence. Because of this requirement, patent practitioners become very proficient at using semicolons and commas. Special legal language is used in drafting the claims and this language has specific meaning. Examples of some legal language used in claim drafting include phrases such as *comprising, consisting of,* and *consisting essentially of.*

> The term **"comprising"** is interpreted as "including the following elements but not excluding others."[10] Practitioners prefer this terminology because it affords the broadest protection.
>
> **"Consisting of"** is interpreted more narrowly than comprising and means "having the recited elements and no more."[11] This phrase affords very narrow protection and is used only when necessary.
>
> **"Consisting essentially of"** falls between "comprising" and "consisting of" and is interpreted as excluding other elements from having any essential significance to the combination.[12] This terminology excludes additional unspecified substances that would affect the basic and novel characteristics of the product defined in the rest of the claim. This phrase is used only when necessary because of the more narrow interpretation.

There are three forms of claims:

(1) independent claims;

(2) dependent claims; and

(3) multiple dependent claims.

These forms are significant for fee purposes and provide scope to the invention. An independent claim stands alone and includes all its necessary limitations. A dependent claim refers to another claim and includes all the limitations of the claim to which it is referring (parent claim) plus the new limitation set forth in the dependent claim. Typically, dependent claims may add additional elements, further describe a limitation in the parent claim, or both. Multiple dependent claims incorporate the limitations of more than one claim where dependent claims incorporate the limitations of one claim. Multiple dependent claims are rarely used in U.S. applications.

Having dependent claims provides *scope* to the invention. Typically, independent claims broadly define the invention. Dependent claims narrow the definition of the invention. Thus, the invention is defined as having a scope ranging from a broad, independent claim, to a narrow, dependent claim. In addition, a narrow, independent claim or picture claim is usually provided to cover the precise invention to be commercialized. Claim scope plays an important role in patent infringement. A defense to patent infringement is to invalidate the patent. To invalidate a patent, the infringer must invalidate each and every claim. Although one may invalidate the broadest claim, there is a chance that the dependent claims will not be invalidated. If only broad claims are presented, the probability of the patent being invalidated is high. However, if a range of claims is presented having varying scope, the chance of the patent being invalidated is less likely. The following example shows how a set of claims provides varying scope for a single invention.

EXAMPLE

I claim:

1. A shaped towpreg ribbon having a cross-section-

al geometry which promotes intimate lateral
contact between adjacent towpreg ribbons having a similar cross-sectional geometry.

2. The shaped towpreg ribbon according to claim 1,
wherein the cross-sectional geometry is selected
from the group consisting of: a triangle, a trapezoid, a parallelogram, and a polygon having more
than 4 sides.

3. The shaped towpreg ribbon according to claim 2,
wherein the cross-sectional geometry is a
triangle.

Figures 7.1 and 7.2 provide a flow chart showing the dependen-
cy of the claims and a diagram showing the claim scope for the invention, respectively.

SPECIFICATION

The **specification** is the part of a patent application
where the invention is disclosed, specified, and described
in detail.

The specification begins with a description of the background
of the invention and concludes with one or more claims directed toward the invention. The specification *describes* the invention. The
claims *define* it. Therefore, the specification is used to interpret the
meaning of the claims. It must meet three requirements[13] to be complete:

(1) It must *describe* the claimed invention (description requirement).

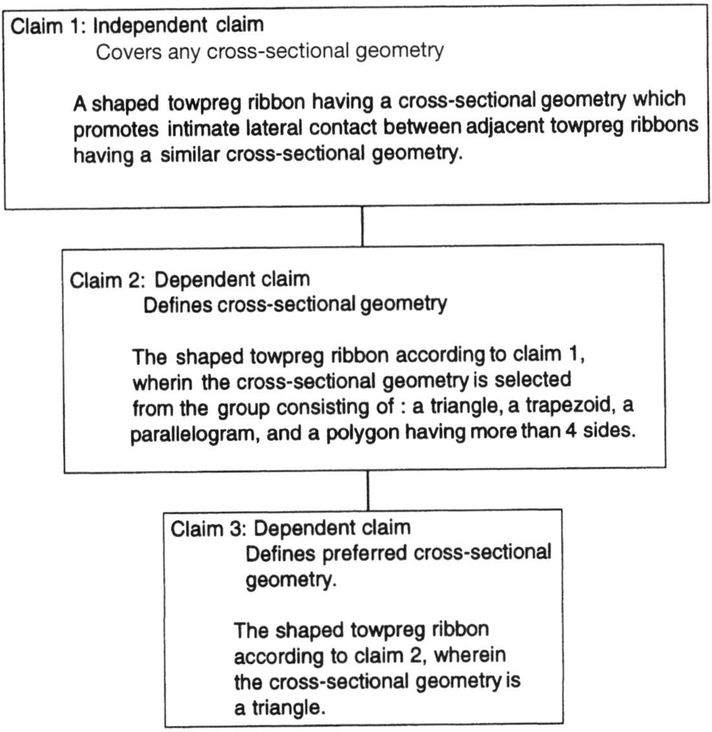

Claim 1: Independent claim
    Covers any cross-sectional geometry

A shaped towpreg ribbon having a cross-sectional geometry which promotes intimate lateral contact between adjacent towpreg ribbons having a similar cross-sectional geometry.

Claim 2: Dependent claim
    Defines cross-sectional geometry

The shaped towpreg ribbon according to claim 1, wherin the cross-sectional geometry is selected from the group consisting of : a triangle, a trapezoid, a parallelogram, and a polygon having more than 4 sides.

Claim 3: Dependent claim
    Defines preferred cross-sectional geometry.

The shaped towpreg ribbon according to claim 2, wherein the cross-sectional geometry is a triangle.

FIGURE 7.1

Claim structure showing independent and dependent claims. Claim 1 is a broad, independent claim. Claim 2 is an intermediate, dependent claim. Claim 3 is a narrow, dependent claim.

(2) The description of the invention must be in full, clear, concise, and exact terms to *enable* any person skilled in the art to which it pertains to make and use the invention (enablement requirement).

(3) It must provide the *best mode* contemplated by the inventor of carrying out the invention at the time the patent application is written (best mode requirement).

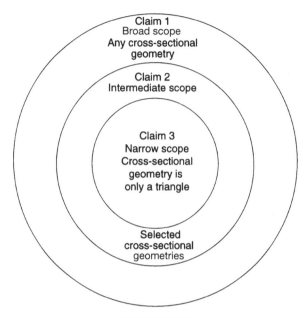

FIGURE 7.2

Claim structure showing how claims vary in scope. Claim 1 is a broad, all-encompassing claim, while claims 2 and 3 fall within the scope of claim 1.

The description requirement assures the public that the inventor had possession of the invention at the time the patent application was filed. This requirement prevents an applicant from trying to later claim an invention that was not originally described in the patent application at the time it was filed. To meet the description requirement, the specification must precisely describe the invention that the applicant wishes to patent in a way that distinguishes it from other inventions and from what is in the public domain. For improvement inventions, the specification focuses on the part or parts of the invention related to the improvement and the specific improvements themselves.

The enablement requirement is met by providing full, clear, concise, and exact terms of the invention so any person skilled in the art relating to the invention or a closely related field can make and use it. This is crucial to having a valid patent. It is the condition of the contract with the government that an inventor must meet to be granted the right to exclude others. As mentioned in Chapter 1, an inventor must decide whether to keep the invention a secret or to patent it. Unfortunately, an inventor cannot have it both ways. The public views patents as stepping stones for further developing technology and increasing the public storehouse of information, and researchers use this information to promote innovation. Withholding this information and yet obtaining the right to exclude others robs society of information that could lead to future innovations.

The best mode requirement goes hand-in-hand with the enablement requirement. The U.S.P.T.O. requires that the inventor describe the invention and the best physical way to make and use it. Merely describing a mode for carrying out the invention is not enough. The inventor must share the best mode known to him or her at the time the patent application is filed. If the inventor discovers a better mode after the patent application is filed, it is not necessary to disclose the better mode. However, if it is discovered that the best mode was withheld from the patent application at the time it was prepared, the requirement is not met and the validity of the patent is in jeopardy.

> *TIP:* Always reveal the best known mode for carrying out the invention.

The patent practitioner drafts the patent specification or *disclosure* with these requirements in mind. The specification begins with a *title* of the invention. The title is as short and specific as possible and describes the claimed invention. Next, if the patent application is claiming the benefit of priority from another pending patent application(s) (either regular or provisional), a statement cross-referencing the patent application to the pending application(s) is included. This statement typically includes the application number(s) and the filing date(s) of the pending application(s) and its relationship to the patent application that is being filed. The statement is inserted under the heading, *Cross-Reference to Related Applications.* If the patent application is not claiming the benefit of priority, then this section is omitted from the patent application and, eventually, the issued patent.

When an invention results from federally sponsored research or development, the specification must contain a statement reflecting this. This statement shows that the U.S. government has a paid-up license in the invention. In addition, the government has the right, in limited circumstances, to require the patent owner to license others on reasonable terms. The government agency usually provides these terms in the contract awarded by them.[14] If the invention did not result from federal funding, this section is deleted.

For computer software related inventions, a microfiche appendix may be necessary to satisfy the description, enablement, and best mode requirements. To save paper, the microfiche appendix contains the computer program listing. A statement is made in the patent application referring to a microfiche appendix and identifying the total number of microfiche and the total number of frames contained in the appendix. If there is no microfiche appendix, this section is omitted.

The background section may or may not contain a statement regarding the field of the invention. The field of the invention is a brief statement describing the subject matter of the claimed invention. The U.S.P.T.O. uses this information to help classify the patent application. The background section usually describes the state of the art, the problems encountered in it, and the previous solutions to these problems. Additional statements may or may not be made regarding the deficiencies in the prior art with respect to solving the problems that the invention solves. These statements usually help to differentiate the invention from that which previously existed.

A summary of the invention is then presented. The summary provides a brief description of the invention describing the exact nature, operation, and purpose of the invention. It also lets the public know exactly what the invention is and what the inventor is claiming as the invention.

When drawings are required to show the invention, a section is added to the specification giving a brief, written description of the views of the drawings. These descriptions are typically no more than one or two sentences long. Not all inventions require drawings. For example, patent applications claiming chemical compositions of matter typically do not contain drawings per se. However, they may contain chemical formulas which are included as text. If no drawings are necessary, this section is omitted.

Following the summary and the description of the drawings is a description of the invention. This description must be in enough detail to enable one skilled in the art to make the invention without extensive experimentation and is written and treated as a dictionary for the claims. The meaning of the claims are interpreted based on this description. A well-written description plays a very important role, especially in patent litigation, and a conscious effort is made to draft this part of the application with the audience in mind. The audience is now considered paramount. In the past, the audience was one of ordinary skill in the art. However, a recent court decision has shifted the audience from one of ordinary skill in the art to a judge in a court of law.[15] Keeping this in mind, an effort is made to explain certain scientific assumptions that, in the past, could safely be left unexplained.

DRAWINGS

A drawing(s) may or may not be required depending on the nature of the claimed invention. If the subject matter of the claimed invention can be understood without a drawing, then no drawing is needed. Drawings simplify the understanding of the invention and are used to satisfy the enablement requirement. The U.S.P.T.O. always requires them for inventions directed toward machines and articles of manufacture. Thus, if a patent application for a machine is submitted to the U.S. P.T.O. without a drawing and no reference is made to a drawing in the specification, the patent application will be considered nonenabling and would have to be refiled. This could be a grave error if there is a statutory bar in effect.

The drawing(s) must show every feature of the invention that the claims specify. When the invention is directed toward an improvement on an old machine, then the U.S.P.T.O. requires several drawings. One drawing must show the improved portion by itself or disconnected from the old structure. Another drawing must only show part of the old machine and how one connects it to the new, improved part or invention. If the drawings do not comply with these requirements, the Examiner will ask for additional illustrations.

The U.S.P.T.O. has specific standards regarding how the drawings are to be prepared. An applicant can submit drawings in black ink (preferred) or in color. Color submissions typically require a petition and an extra fee. Photographs are generally not acceptable. However, there are certain cases when the U.S.P.T.O. will allow them. In addition, the U.S.P.T.O. has certain requirements with respect to:

- paper;
- margins;
- shading; and
- presentation and arrangement of the views.

Patent drawings are not drawn in the same manner as traditional engineering or architectural drawings. The U.S.P.T.O. is very particular about the patent drawings and publishes a one-half-inch-thick book containing rules and examples relating to patent drawings.[16] Because of the specialized nature of patent drawings, it is usually necessary to employ the services of a patent draftsperson to prepare the drawings.

ABSTRACT

The **abstract** is a general description of the technical disclosure provided in the specification.

The purpose of the abstract is to enable the U.S.P.T.O. and the public to quickly learn the gist of the disclosure. The abstract is not used to interpret the meaning of the claims. Although the abstract appears on the front page of the issued patent, it is submitted as the last page of the patent application.

Review

Employing the assistance of a patent practitioner goes beyond preparing the patent application. The inventor benefits from the practitioner's experience working with the people and being familiar with the system at the U.S.P.T.O. Being properly prepared and having the information the patent practitioner needs to prepare the patent application maximizes the efficiency of the time spent preparing the patent application and will ultimately save money with respect to the practitioner's fees.

Every utility patent application contains, at a minimum, a background section, a summary, a detailed description, at least one claim and an abstract. Each of these sections is completed specifically for the invention. The claims are the most important part of the patent application and are what the Examiner looks at to determine whether the invention is new, useful, and not obvious. The practitioner considers these requirements when drafting the claims and preparing the rest of the patent application. Once the patent application is prepared, it is ready to be filed in the U.S.P.T.O.

Annotated References

1. U.S.P.T.O., Office of Enrollment and Discipline, (1997). "General Requirements for Admission to the Examination for Registration to Practice In Patent Cases Before the U.S. Patent and Trademark Office," U.S. Department of Commerce, Washington, D.C. *(Requirements for taking the patent bar examination.)*

2. UMC Electronics v. United States, 816 F.2d 647,656, 2 U.S.P.Q.2d 1465, 1472 (Fed. Cir. 1987). *(Case setting precedent for disclosure of invention in a proposal constituting an offer for sale.)*

3. 35 U.S.C. § 101. *(Statute relating to utility.)*

4. 35 U.S.C. § 102. *(Statute relating to novelty.)*

5. 35 U.S.C. § 103. *(Statute relating to nonobviousness.)*

6. Reliance Novelty Corp. v. Dworzek, 80 F. 902 (N.D. Cal. 1897). *(Example of an invention considered as harmful to the public.)*

7. Structural Rubber Products Co. v. Park Rubber Co., 749 F.2d 707, 223 U.S.P.Q. (BNA) 1264 (Fed. Cir. 1984). *(Example of anticipation relying on a single prior art reference.)*

8. Environmental Designs, Ltd. v. Union Oil Co. of Cal., 713 F.2d 693, 696-97, 218 U.S.P.Q. 865, 868-69 (Fed. Cir. 1983). *(Defining the level of ordinary skill in the art.)*

9. In re Soni, 54 F.3d 746, 34 U.S.P.Q.2d 1684 (Fed. Cir. 1995). *(Example of nonobviousness.)*

10. Moleculon Research Corp. v. CBS, Inc., 229 U.S.P.Q. (BNA) 805, 812 (Fed. Cir. 1986). *(Interpretation of the phrase "comprising".)*

11. In re Certain Slide Fastener Stringers, 216 U.S.P.Q. (BNA) 907 (U.S. Int. Tr. Comm. 1981). *(Interpretation of the phrase "consisting of".)*

12. Special Metals Corp. v. Teledyne Industries, Inc., 219 U.S.P.Q. (BNA) 953 (4th Cir. 1983). *(Interpretation of the phrase "consisting essentially of".)*

13. 35 U.S.C. § 112, first paragraph. *(Statutory basis for the specification.)*

14. Manual of Patent Examining Procedure section 310. *(Government license rights to inventions made under federally sponsored research.)*

15. Markman v. Westview Instruments, Inc., 52 F.3d 967, 34 U.S.P.Q.2d 1321 (Fed.Cir. 1995). *(Precedent for claim interpretation is a matter of law. This provides the basis that the specification should be written considering the audience to be a judge rather than one of ordinary skill in the art.)*

16. U.S. Department of Commerce Patent and Trademark Office (October 1997),"Guide for the Preparation of Patent Drawings", U.S. Government Printing Office.

8

Filing and Prosecuting the Patent Application

Once the patent application is prepared, it is ready to be sent or filed in the U.S.P.T.O. along with various formal papers that complete the filing process. After the application is filed, it is examined to determine whether the invention is patentable. This chapter looks at this process.

Filing the Patent Application

When a patent application is filed, it typically has *formal papers* that are executed by the inventor that accompany it.

The **formal papers** are additional papers submitted along with the patent application when filing in the U.S.P.T.O.

Four kinds of formal papers exist:

(1) oath or declaration by the inventor;

(2) power of attorney (may be combined with the oath or declaration);

(3) assignment; and

(4) a small entity statement.

Whether or not all of these papers are submitted depends upon the circumstances surrounding the filing of the application. For example, if the inventor is filing the patent application on his or her own, then there will be no power of attorney form. If there is no transfer of ownership from the inventor to another entity, then no assignment will be filed, or if the party that will ultimately own or have interest in the invention is not a small entity, then the small entity statement will not be filed. The one paper that is always filed with a patent application is the oath or declaration by the inventor. The U.S.P.T.O. requires this paper to complete every patent application filing.

OATH OR DECLARATION BY THE INVENTOR AND POWER OF ATTORNEY

The **oath or declaration by the inventor** is a statement made by the inventor that he or she believes to be the original and first inventor of the invention claimed in the patent application.[1] The oath or declaration also provides the inventor's address and country of citizenship. Lastly, the inventor declares that statements made in the application are true.

The statement made by the inventor may be either an oath or a declaration. The difference between an oath and a declaration is that an oath must be executed before an authorized official of the U.S. such as a notary public, while a declaration does not require a notary's signature. However, the declaration must contain an acknowledgment that the statements made by the person signing are true and that willful false statements are punishable by fine or imprisonment and may jeopardize the validity of the application or any patent that issues from it. Typically, a declaration is filed instead of an oath.

Figure 8.1 gives an example of a declaration form for a utility or design patent application. The declaration contains four main sections. In the first section (section A), the inventor(s) states that he or she believes that he or she is the original, first, and sole (or joint) inventor of the subject matter claimed in the patent application. For identification purposes, the title of the invention is provided along with the filing date and application number if they are available. The inventor also states that the contents of the application, including the claims, have been reviewed and that the inventor acknowledges the duty to disclose information which is material to patentability of the invention. This section thus accomplishes the following four functions:

(1) The inventor declares that he or she believes to be the original, first, and sole (or joint) inventor of the claimed invention.

(2) The specification is identified.

(3) The inventor states that the specification, including the claims, has been reviewed and is understood by him or her.

(4) The inventor acknowledges the duty to disclose information which is material to patentability.

Please type a plus sign (+) inside this box → ☐

PTO/SB/01 (12-97)
Approved for use through 9/30/00. OMB 0651-0032
Patent and Trademark Office; U.S. DEPARTMENT OF COMMERCE
Under the Paperwork Reduction Act of 1995, no persons are required to respond to a collection of information unless it contains a valid OMB control number.

DECLARATION FOR UTILITY OR DESIGN PATENT APPLICATION (37 CFR 1.63)	Attorney Docket Number	
	First Named Inventor	
	COMPLETE IF KNOWN	
	Application Number	/
☐ Declaration Submitted with Initial Filing OR ☐ Declaration Submitted after Initial Filing (surcharge (37 CFR 1.16 (e)) required)	Filing Date	
	Group Art Unit	
	Examiner Name	

A

As a below named inventor, I hereby declare that:

My residence, post office address, and citizenship are as stated below next to my name.

I believe I am the original, first and sole inventor (if only one name is listed below) or an original, first and joint inventor (if plural names are listed below) of the subject matter which is claimed and for which a patent is sought on the invention entitled:

the specification of which
☐ is attached hereto   *(Title of the Invention)*
OR
☐ was filed on (MM/DD/YYYY) [   ] as United States Application Number or PCT International

Application Number [   ] and was amended on (MM/DD/YYYY) [   ] (if applicable).

I hereby state that I have reviewed and understand the contents of the above identified specification, including the claims, as amended by any amendment specifically referred to above.

I acknowledge the duty to disclose information which is material to patentability as defined in 37 CFR 1.56.

B

I hereby claim foreign priority benefits under 35 U.S.C. 119(a)-(d) or 365(b) of any foreign application(s) for patent or inventor's certificate, or 365(a) of any PCT international application which designated at least one country other than the United States of America, listed below and have also identified below, by checking the box, any foreign application for patent or inventor's certificate, or of any PCT international application having a filing date before that of the application on which priority is claimed.

Prior Foreign Application Number(s)	Country	Foreign Filing Date (MM/DD/YYYY)	Priority Not Claimed	Certified Copy Attached? YES	NO
			☐	☐	☐
			☐	☐	☐
			☐	☐	☐
			☐	☐	☐

☐ Additional foreign application numbers are listed on a supplemental priority data sheet PTO/SB/02B attached hereto.

I hereby claim the benefit under 35 U.S.C. 119(e) of any United States provisional application(s) listed below.

Application Number(s)	Filing Date (MM/DD/YYYY)	
		☐ Additional provisional application numbers are listed on a supplemental priority data sheet PTO/SB/02B attached hereto.

[Page 1 of 2]

Burden Hour Statement: This form is estimated to take 0.4 hours to complete. Time will vary depending upon the needs of the individual case. Any comments on the amount of time you are required to complete this form should be sent to the Chief Information Officer, Patent and Trademark Office, Washington, DC 20231. DO NOT SEND FEES OR COMPLETED FORMS TO THIS ADDRESS. SEND TO: Assistant Commissioner for Patents, Washington, DC 20231.

FIGURE 8.1 *(continues)*

Declaration for a utility or design patent application. Section A gives the inventor's statement. Section B is where priority from another applica-

PTO/SB/01 (12-97)
Approved for use through 9/30/00. OMB 0651-0032
Patent and Trademark Office; U.S. DEPARTMENT OF COMMERCE
Under the Paperwork Reduction Act of 1995, no persons are required to respond to a collection of information unless it contains a valid OMB control number.

Please type a plus sign (+) inside this box →

DECLARATION — Utility or Design Patent Application

I hereby claim the benefit under 35 U.S.C. 120 of any United States application(s), or 365(c) of any PCT international application designating the United States of America, listed below and, insofar as the subject matter of each of the claims of this application is not disclosed in the prior United States or PCT International application in the manner provided by the first paragraph of 35 U.S.C. 112, I acknowledge the duty to disclose information which is material to patentability as defined in 37 CFR 1.56 which became available between the filing date of the prior application and the national or PCT international filing date of this application.

B

U.S. Parent Application or PCT Parent Number	Parent Filing Date (MM/DD/YYYY)	Parent Patent Number (if applicable)

☐ Additional U.S. or PCT international application numbers are listed on a supplemental priority data sheet PTO/SB/02B attached hereto.

As a named inventor, I hereby appoint the following registered practitioner(s) to prosecute this application and to transact all business in the Patent and Trademark Office connected therewith: ☐ Customer Number _____→ *Place Customer Number Bar Code Label here*
OR
☐ Registered practitioner(s) name/registration number listed below

C

Name	Registration Number	Name	Registration Number

☐ Additional registered practitioner(s) named on supplemental Registered Practitioner Information sheet PTO/SB/02C attached hereto.

Direct all correspondence to: ☐ Customer Number or Bar Code Label _____ OR ☐ Correspondence address below

Name	
Address	
Address	

City		State		ZIP	
Country		Telephone		Fax	

I hereby declare that all statements made herein of my own knowledge are true and that all statements made on information and belief are believed to be true; and further that these statements were made with the knowledge that willful false statements and the like so made are punishable by fine or imprisonment, or both, under 18 U.S.C. 1001 and that such willful false statements may jeopardize the validity of the application or any patent issued thereon.

D

Name of Sole or First Inventor:	☐ A petition has been filed for this unsigned inventor
Given Name (first and middle [if any])	Family Name or Surname

Inventor's Signature			Date	
Residence: City		State	Country	Citizenship
Post Office Address				
Post Office Address				
City	State	ZIP	Country	

☐ Additional inventors are being named on the _____ supplemental Additional Inventor(s) sheet(s) PTO/SB/02A attached hereto

[Page 2 of 2]

FIGURE 8.1 *(continued)*

tion is claimed. Section C serves as the power of attorney. Section D is the inventor's declaration and signature.

Section B allows the inventor to claim priority from:

(1) any foreign patent applications or inventor's certificates;

(2) provisional patent applications, and/or previously filed and still pending U.S. patent applications; or

(3) PCT applications.

Section C serves as a *power of attorney* where the inventor appoints a registered patent practitioner to be his or her representative in the U.S.P.T.O. The practitioner's contact information and registration number are inserted in this section. Although the power of attorney is typically a part of the declaration, it may also be filed as a separate paper.

Section D provides the inventor's full name, residence, and country of citizenship. In addition the inventor signs this section declaring that all statements made are true or believed to be true.

Typically, sections A–D are completed by the patent practitioner, with the exception of the inventor's signature. That is why this information needs to be provided to the practitioner. Before this form is completed, the correct inventorship must be determined.

Inventorship is different from *ownership*. Inventorship is based on how the invention is claimed. An inventor is a person who contributed to the concept of the subject matter of at least one claim in the patent application. Conversely, a person who merely follows the instructions of another and does not contribute to the claimed invention is not an inventor.

> An **inventor** is a person who contributed to the concept of at least one claim in a patent application.

Ownership has nothing to do with inventorship. Ownership relates to having the right to enforce or license the patent. A person can be an inventor without owning the invention. Conversely, an entity, like a company, can own a patent without being the inventor. This transfer of ownership takes place through an assignment (discussed later in this section).

When a single person is responsible for the contribution to every claim in a patent application, he or she is a sole inventor. When several individuals collaborate and contribute to the subject matter of the claims, they are joint inventors. However, it is not necessary for each of the inventors to contribute to the subject matter of each claim.

EXAMPLE

Cheryl and Fred work for XYZ company. Fred developed a way to make a chair recline using a button installed on the side of the chair. Cheryl thought Fred's button was a good idea but she had injured her back and found that having to lean over to push the button on the side of the chair hurt her back. To overcome this problem, Cheryl invented a way to activate the button without having to lean over. A patent application was prepared claiming both Fred's button and Cheryl's method for activating the button without having to lean over. Thus, although Cheryl and Fred did not contribute to the subject matter for each claim they are still coinventors because the claims included both of their contributions to the invention.

Note that in the example, Cheryl improved on Fred's invention. This is different from merely executing someone's orders. A lab technician who does exactly what he or she is told to do is not a coinventor.[2] Similarly, a supervisor or employer of an inventor is not a coinventor merely because he or she is a supervisor or employer. There must be a contribution to the claimed invention.

> *WARNING:* To qualify as an inventor, one must contribute to the *claimed* invention.

The U.S.P.T.O. is fairly forgiving with respect to naming the wrong inventors on a patent application. If one discovers that there is someone named on the application or issued patent that should not be or that someone was accidentally left off the patent, filing a petition and paying a fee may correct the mistake. The inventorship can be corrected anytime after the mistake is discovered. However, failing to correct the inventorship once an error has been made apparent could result in the patent being invalidated if this were discovered during litigation.

ASSIGNMENT

A patent is treated as a piece of property which is owned. The inventor is always the original owner and holds the title to the invention. However, an inventor may transfer all or part of the ownership to another individual or to an entity such as a business or university in exchange for a sum of money or other valuable consideration. Whoever is the owner of the patent is the one who has the right to license the patent and to sue infringers. Thus, transferring the title or ownership of a patent should not be treated lightly.

> An **assignment** of a patent is the transfer of ownership in either an invention or a patent from the inventor to an-

other party in exchange for a sum of money or other valuable consideration.

An assignment may result in the transfer of:

(1) all exclusive rights in the patent;

(2) an undivided portion or a percentage interest; or

(3) all rights within a certain specified region of the United States.

Typically, an employed inventor has an obligation to assign or transfer the title in the invention to the employer. A common corporate practice is to have a new employee sign an employment agreement that states that the employee agrees to assign all rights to inventions made in certain circumstances to the company. Usually, the contract explains the circumstances.

> *TIP:* If you are required to sign an employment agreement, check it to see what the terms are regarding ownership of inventions.

Assignments also extend to the academic community. Most academic institutions have intellectual property policies that explain the ownership of inventions resulting from academic research.

> *TIP:* If you are employed by an academic institution, check your institution's intellectual property policy regarding ownership of inventions resulting from academic research.

Co-ownership occurs when an invention that results from a joint research activity must be assigned to two different entities.

This situation is often frowned upon because an exclusive license cannot be offered to a third party, nor can the invention be used exclusively by one co-owner without the permission of the other co-owner.

EXAMPLE

Rob works for XYZ company. Anne works for the College of William and Mary. Together, Rob and Anne invent a device for dampening sound. Since Rob is an employee of XYZ company, he is under an obligation to assign his invention to XYZ company. Anne has an obligation to assign her invention to the College of William and Mary. Because of their collaborative effort, both the College of William and Mary and XYZ company own the patent. If XYZ company decides it wants to have exclusive rights to the patent to block competitors from entering the market, XYZ company should license the other half of the patent from the College of William and Mary.

Assignment of an invention or patent may take place anytime by executing an assignment agreement. This is a contractual agreement between the inventor and the party to which the inventor is making the transfer. Figure 8.2 shows an example of an assignment for a patent application. The assignment typically identifies the inventor, the title of the invention, the application filing date, and the application number (if available). In addition, the assignment identifies the party to whom the transfer is being made and the agreed upon sum being paid to the inventor. The inventor signs the document and, although it is not necessary, it may be notarized.

ASSIGNMENT OF APPLICATION	Docket Number (Optional)

Whereas, I, _____ of _____, hereafter referred to as applicant, have invented certain new and useful improvements in _____

_____

☐ for which an application for a United States Patent was filed on _____,
Application Number _____/_____.

☐ for which an application for a United States Patent was executed on _____, and

Whereas, _____ of _____ herein referred to "assignee" whose post office address is _____ is desirous of acquiring the entire right, title and interest in the same;

Now, therefore, in consideration of the sum of _____ dollars ($_____), the receipt whereof is acknowledged, and other good and valuable consideration, I, the applicant, by these presents do sell, assign and transfer unto said assignee the full and exclusive right to the said invention in the United States and the entire right, title and interest in and to any and all Patents which may be granted therefor in the United States, I hereby authorize and request the Commissioner of Patents and Trademarks to issue said United States Patent to said assignee, of the entire right, title, and interest in and to the same, for his sole use and behoof; and for the use and behoof of his legal representatives, to the full end of the term for which said Patent may be granted, as fully and entirely as the same would have been held by me had this assignment and sale not been made.

Executed this _____ day of _____, 19_____,

at _____.

_____
(Signature)

State of _____) SS:
County of _____)
Before me personally appeared said _____
and acknowledged the foregoing instrument to be his free act and deed this _____
day of _____, 19_____.

Seal

_____
(Notary Public)

FIGURE 8.2

A patent application assignment. Note the section stating that the applicant sells, assigns and transfers to the assignee the full and exclusive right to the invention.

SMALL ENTITY STATEMENT

The U.S.P.T.O. offers a 50% discount on most of their fees for applicants who qualify under small entity status. Typical small entities include:

- independent inventors
- nonprofit organizations
- small business concerns.

The small entity does not have to be in the U.S. to qualify for the reduced fees. The only requirement is that the small entity may not assign, grant, convey, or license (or be under an obligation to do so) the rights in the invention to a large entity. Once this occurs, the small entity status is lost and the U.S.P.T.O. must be notified.

A **small entity** is an independent inventor, nonprofit organization, or small business concern that qualifies for a 50% reduction on U.S.P.T.O. fees.

INDEPENDENT INVENTORS

An **independent inventor** is an individual who has not assigned, granted, conveyed, or licensed any rights in the invention to any person or concern who would not qualify as a small entity. In addition, the independent inventor is not under an obligation under contract or law to do so.

Figure 8.3 provides an example of a small entity statement for an independent inventor. Note that small entity status may be claimed when the patent is initially filed, while it is pending, or after it has issued. In the small entity statement, the inventor (or joint in-

PTO/SB/09 (12-97)
Approved for use through 9/30/00. OMB 0651-0031
Patent and Trademark Office; U.S. DEPARTMENT OF COMMERCE
Under the Paperwork Reduction Act of 1995, no persons are required to respond to a collection of information unless it displays a valid OMB control number.

STATEMENT CLAIMING SMALL ENTITY STATUS (37 CFR 1.9(f) & 1.27(b))--INDEPENDENT INVENTOR	Docket Number (Optional)

Applicant, Patentee, or Identifier: _____

Application or Patent No.: _____

Filed or Issued: _____

Title: _____

A

As a below named inventor, I hereby state that I qualify as an independent inventor as defined in 37 CFR 1.9(c) for purposes of paying reduced fees to the Patent and Trademark Office described in:

☐ the specification filed herewith with title as listed above.

☐ the application identified above.

☐ the patent identified above.

B

I have not assigned, granted, conveyed, or licensed, and am under no obligation under contract or law to assign, grant, convey, or license, any rights in the invention to any person who would not qualify as an independent inventor under 37 CFR 1.9(c) if that person had made the invention, or to any concern which would not qualify as a small business concern under 37 CFR 1.9(d) or a nonprofit organization under 37 CFR 1.9(e).

Each person, concern, or organization to which I have assigned, granted, conveyed, or licensed or am under an obligation under contract or law to assign, grant, convey, or license any rights in the invention is listed below:

☐ No such person, concern, or organization exists.

☐ Each such person, concern, or organization is listed below.

Separate statements are required from each named person, concern, or organization having rights to the invention stating their status as small entities. (37 CFR 1.27)

C

I acknowledge the duty to file, in this application or patent, notification of any change in status resulting in loss of entitlement to small entity status prior to paying, or at the time of paying, the earliest of the issue fee or any maintenance fee due after the date on which status as a small entity is no longer appropriate. (37 CFR 1.28(b))

NAME OF INVENTOR	NAME OF INVENTOR	NAME OF INVENTOR
Signature of inventor	Signature of inventor	Signature of inventor
Date	Date	Date

Burden Hour Statement: This form is estimated to take 0.2 hours to complete. Time will vary depending upon the needs of the individual case. Any comments on the amount of time you are required to complete this form should be sent to the Chief Information Officer, Patent and Trademark Office, Washington, DC 20231. DO NOT SEND FEES OR COMPLETED FORMS TO THIS ADDRESS. SEND TO: Assistant Commissioner for Patents, Washington, DC 20231.

FIGURE 8.3

Small entity statement for an independent inventor. Section A states the qualification as an independent inventor. Section B identifies whether any transfer or obligation to transfer rights has occurred. Section C is an acknowledgment of the duty to notify the U.S.P.T.O. of any change in status.

ventors) states that he or she qualifies as an independent inventor. In addition, if the inventor is under an obligation under contract or law to, or has assigned, granted, conveyed, or licensed the rights in the invention to another small entity, that entity must be listed. The inventor also must acknowledge the duty to file, either in the application or patent, a notice of any change in status that would result in a loss of small entity status before paying or at the time of paying either the issue fee or any maintenance fee whichever is due after small entity status is no longer appropriate. Lastly, each inventor must sign the statement.

NONPROFIT ORGANIZATIONS

There are several types of organizations that qualify as nonprofit organizations for the purposes of paying reduced fees in the U.S.P.T.O. These organizations include:

- universities or other institutions of higher education
- organizations tax exempt under IRS code (26 U.S.C. 501(a) and 501(c)(3))
- nonprofit scientific or educational under a U.S. state statute
- foreign organizations that would qualify as tax exempt if they were located in the U.S.
- foreign organizations that would qualify as nonprofit scientific or educational under a U.S. state statute if they were located in the U.S.

A **nonprofit organization** is an institution of higher education, an organization that meets the qualifications for an IRS-defined tax-exempt nonprofit organization, or a nonprofit scientific or educational organization.

Figure 8.4 shows an example of a small entity statement for a nonprofit organization. This statement differs from the independent inventor statement in several ways. First, an official having the power to act for the nonprofit organization executes the statement. Second, the document states that the rights have been conveyed to and remain with the nonprofit organization. Note that if the rights are not exclusive, the other concern must also file a small entity statement. As with the independent inventor statement, the official must also acknowledge the duty to file a notification of any change in the status.

SMALL BUSINESS CONCERN

A **small business concern** is an entity that has less than 500 employees, including those of its affiliates.

Figure 8.5 provides a small entity statement for a small business concern. Either the owner of the small business concern or an official empowered to act for the concern signs the statement. The person signing the document states that the small business concern qualifies as a small business. Note that the number of employees is the determining factor and that this number is the average, over the previous fiscal year of the concern, of the persons employed on a full-time, part-time, or temporary basis during each of the pay periods of the fiscal year. An affiliate is defined by who controls it. If one concern controls or has the power to control the other, or a third party or parties controls or has the power to control both, the entity is an affiliate. As with the other small entity statements, if the rights held by the concern are not exclusive, the other concerns having rights must also be listed and separate statements provided. Lastly, the person signing must acknowledge the duty to file a notification of any change in status.

Filing and Prosecuting the Patent Application

PTO/SB/11 (12-97)
Approved for use through 9/30/00. OMB 0651-0031
Patent and Trademark Office; U.S. DEPARTMENT OF COMMERCE
Under the Paperwork Reduction Act of 1995, no persons are required to respond to a collection of information unless it displays a valid OMB control number.

STATEMENT CLAIMING SMALL ENTITY STATUS (37 CFR 1.9(f) & 1.27(d))--NONPROFIT ORGANIZATION	Docket Number (Optional)

Applicant, Patentee, or Identifier: _____
Application or Patent No.: _____
Filed or Issued: _____
Title: _____

I hereby state that I am an official empowered to act on behalf of the nonprofit organization identified below:
  NAME OF NONPROFIT ORGANIZATION _____
  ADDRESS OF NONPROFIT ORGANIZATION _____

A

TYPE OF NONPROFIT ORGANIZATION:
☐ UNIVERSITY OR OTHER INSTITUTION OF HIGHER EDUCATION

☐ TAX EXEMPT UNDER INTERNAL REVENUE SERVICE CODE (26 U.S.C. 501(a) and 501(c)(3))

☐ NONPROFIT SCIENTIFIC OR EDUCATIONAL UNDER STATUTE OF STATE OF THE UNITED STATES OF AMERICA
   (NAME OF STATE _____)
   (CITATION OF STATUTE _____)

☐ WOULD QUALIFY AS TAX EXEMPT UNDER INTERNAL REVENUE SERVICE CODE (26 U.S.C. 501(a) and 501(c)(3))
   IF LOCATED IN THE UNITED STATES OF AMERICA

☐ WOULD QUALIFY AS NONPROFIT SCIENTIFIC OR EDUCATIONAL UNDER STATUTE OF STATE OF THE UNITED
   STATES OF AMERICA IF LOCATED IN THE UNITED STATES OF AMERICA
   (NAME OF STATE _____)
   (CITATION OF STATUTE _____)

   I hereby state that the nonprofit organization identified above qualifies as a nonprofit organization as defined in 37 CFR 1.9(e) for purposes of paying reduced fees to the United States Patent and Trademark Office regarding the invention described in:

   ☐ the specification filed herewith with title as listed above.
   ☐ the application identified above.
   ☐ the patent identified above.

B

   I hereby state that rights under contract or law have been conveyed to and remain with the nonprofit organization regarding the above identified invention. If the rights held by the nonprofit organization are not exclusive, each individual, concern, or organization having rights in the invention must file separate statements as to their status as small entities and that no rights to the invention are held by any person, other than the inventor, who would not qualify as an independent inventor under 37 CFR 1.9(c) if that person made the invention, or by any concern which would not qualify as a small business concern under 37 CFR 1.9(d) or a nonprofit organization under 37 CFR 1.9(e).

   Each person, concern, or organization having any rights in the invention is listed below:

   ☐ no such person, concern, or organization exists.
   ☐ each such person, concern, or organization is listed below.

C

   I acknowledge the duty to file, in this application or patent, notification of any change in status resulting in loss of entitlement to small entity status prior to paying, or at the time of paying, the earliest of the issue fee or any maintenance fee due after the date on which status as a small entity is no longer appropriate. (37 CFR 1.28(b))

NAME OF PERSON SIGNING _____

TITLE IN ORGANIZATION OF PERSON SIGNING _____

ADDRESS OF PERSON SIGNING _____

SIGNATURE _____ DATE _____

Burden Hour Statement: This form is estimated to take 0.2 hours to complete. Time will vary depending upon the needs of the individual case. Any comments on the amount of time you are required to complete this form should be sent to the Chief Information Officer, Patent and Trademark Office, Washington, DC 20231. DO NOT SEND FEES OR COMPLETED FORMS TO THIS ADDRESS. SEND TO: Assistant Commissioner for Patents, Washington, DC 20231.

FIGURE 8.4

Small entity statement for a nonprofit organization. Section A identifies the type of nonprofit organization. Section B identifies whether any transfer or obligation to transfer rights has occurred. Section C is signed by an official of the organization.

PTO/SB/10 (12-97)
Approved for use through 9/30/00. OMB 0651-0031
Patent and Trademark Office; U.S. DEPARTMENT OF COMMERCE
Under the Paperwork Reduction Act of 1995, no persons are required to respond to a collection of information unless it displays a valid OMB control number.

STATEMENT CLAIMING SMALL ENTITY STATUS (37 CFR 1.9(f) & 1.27(c))–SMALL BUSINESS CONCERN	Docket Number (Optional)

Applicant, Patentee, or Identifier: _____

Application or Patent No.: _____

Filed or Issued: _____

Title: _____

I hereby state that I am
- ☐ the owner of the small business concern identified below:
- ☐ an official of the small business concern empowered to act on behalf of the concern identified below:

A {

NAME OF SMALL BUSINESS CONCERN _____

ADDRESS OF SMALL BUSINESS CONCERN _____

_____

B {

I hereby state that the above identified small business concern qualifies as a small business concern as defined in 13 CFR Part 121 for purposes of paying reduced fees to the United States Patent and Trademark Office, in that the number of employees of the concern, including those of its affiliates, does not exceed 500 persons. For purposes of this statement, (1) the number of employees of the business concern is the average over the previous fiscal year of the concern of the persons employed on a full-time, part-time, or temporary basis during each of the pay periods of the fiscal year, and (2) concerns are affiliates of each other when either, directly or indirectly, one concern controls or has the power to control the other, or a third party or parties controls or has the power to control both.

I hereby state that rights under contract or law have been conveyed to and remain with the small business concern identified above with regard to the invention described in:

- ☐ the specification filed herewith with title as listed above.
- ☐ the application identified above.
- ☐ the patent identified above.

If the rights held by the above identified small business concern are not exclusive, each individual, concern, or organization having rights in the invention must file separate statements as to their status as small entities, and no rights to the invention are held by any person, other than the inventor, who would not qualify as an independent inventor under 37 CFR 1.9(c) if that person made the invention, or by any concern which would not qualify as a small business concern under 37 CFR 1.9(d), or a nonprofit organization under 37 CFR 1.9(e).

Each person, concern, or organization having any rights in the invention is listed below:
- ☐ no such person, concern, or organization exists.
- ☐ each such person, concern, or organization is listed below.

Separate statements are required from each named person, concern or organization having rights to the invention stating their status as small entities. (37 CFR 1.27)

C {

I acknowledge the duty to file, in this application or patent, notification of any change in status resulting in loss of entitlement to small entity status prior to paying, or at the time of paying, the earliest of the issue fee or any maintenance fee due after the date on which status as a small entity is no longer appropriate. (37 CFR 1.28(b))

NAME OF PERSON SIGNING _____

TITLE OF PERSON IF OTHER THAN OWNER _____

ADDRESS OF PERSON SIGNING _____

SIGNATURE _____ DATE _____

Burden Hour Statement: This form is estimated to take 0.2 hours to complete. Time will vary depending upon the needs of the individual case. Any comments on the amount of time you are required to complete this form should be sent to the Chief Information Officer, Patent and Trademark Office, Washington, DC 20231. DO NOT SEND FEES OR COMPLETED FORMS TO THIS ADDRESS. SEND TO: Assistant Commissioner for Patents, Washington, DC 20231.

FIGURE 8.5

Small entity statement for a small business concern. Section A identifies the small business concern. Section B states that the small business concern qualifies as such. Section C is signed by an official or owner of the small business concern.

The Information Disclosure Statement

Usually, an *information disclosure statement* will accompany the patent application along with the formal papers at the time of filing. The U.S.P.T.O. requires each individual associated with the filing and prosecution of a patent application to disclose to the U.S.P.T.O. all information known to the individual to be *material to the patentability of the invention*.[3] This duty exists for every claim in the invention. If this duty to disclose is violated through bad faith or intentional misconduct, no patent will be granted. Usually this type of misconduct is discovered during litigation.

> **Information material to patentability** is information that establishes by itself or in combination with other information, a *prima facie* case of unpatentability of a claim. In addition, if the information refutes or is inconsistent with a position the applicant takes in opposing an argument of unpatentability relied on by the U.S.P.T.O., or asserts an argument of patentability, it is material.[4]

> A **prima facie** case of unpatentability is established when the information compels a conclusion that a claim is unpatentable under the preponderance of evidence, burden-of-proof standard, giving each term in the claim its broadest reasonable construction consistent with the specification, and before any consideration is given to evidence which may be submitted in an attempt to establish a contrary conclusion of patentability.[5]

The types of information submitted may include:

- prior art cited in search reports of a foreign patent office in a counterpart application; and

- the closest information over which individuals associated with the filing or prosecution of a patent application believe any pending claim patentably defines.[6]

Usually, this information is found in references and issued patents. Sometimes the information is contained in a company's product literature or it exists as confidential business information. Not yet issued copending related patent applications are also considered material. Whatever its form, if the information is known to anyone involved with the application, it must be submitted to the U.S.P.T.O. The individuals associated with the filing or prosecution of a patent application include:

- each inventor named in the application;

- each patent practitioner who prepares or prosecutes the application;

- other people who are substantively involved with preparing or prosecuting the application and who are associated with the inventor, the assignee, or those to whom there is an obligation to assign the application.[7]

WARNING: Intentionally failing to submit information that may be material to patentability is considered as a commitment of fraud on the U.S.P.T.O. and will result in an unenforceable patent.

TIP: If you are aware of any references that may affect the patentability of any of the claims in your patent application, make sure your practitioner knows about them.

Patent Pending Status

Once the patent application is prepared and the formal papers have been executed, it is ready to be filed in the U.S.P.T.O. There are several ways the application may be filed:

(1) It may be sent to the U.S.P.T.O. by regular U.S. mail.

(2) It may be sent to the U.S.P.T.O. by the U.S. Postal Service Express Mail to Addressee.

(3) It may be hand delivered to the U.S.P.T.O.

The filing date of a patent application is the date on which the U.S.P.T.O. *receives* the application. If there is a statutory bar date that is quickly approaching, filing the application by regular U.S. mail is not recommended. However, filing an application by Express Mail and using an Express Mail certificate will afford the application a filing date as of the date the application is *mailed* to the U.S.P.T.O. This is especially beneficial if the application must get to the U.S.P.T.O. before a statutory bar date and hand delivery is not an option. Most practitioners file their patent applications using an Express Mail certificate. Besides obtaining the earliest possible filing date, Express Mail makes it possible to track the application if it gets lost. Once the patent application is filed and the U.S.P.T.O. receives it, the invention may be marked as "patent pending."

Patent Pending is a phrase marked on a product indicating that a patent application has been filed for the product and that the patent application has claims that cover the product.

When a person marks a product patent pending, he or she is letting potential infringers know that a patent has been applied for and that the patent may issue anytime. Marking an item patent pending *does not* offer an applicant the right to exclude others from making, using, selling, or importing the invention. Only an issued patent will provide this right. Therefore, marking an item patent pending only serves as a warning to potential infringers that a patent may issue soon. It is unlawful to mark an item as patent pending or patent applied for when, in fact, there is no patent pending. If this is done with the intention of deceiving the public, this type of deceit is punishable with a fine of up to $500 per offense.[8]

> *WARNING:* Never mark an item patent pending if you have not applied for a patent.

> *WARNING:* Marking an item patent pending does not provide any rights to exclude others from making, using, selling, or importing the invention in the U.S.

When the U.S.P.T.O. receives the patent application, it is reviewed to make sure that all the papers are in order and an application number (or serial number) and a filing date are assigned to it. A filing receipt (Fig. 8.6) is then sent to the patent practitioner. It usually takes about 8 to 12 weeks from the time the patent application is mailed to the U.S.P.T.O. to receive the filing receipt. The filing receipt serves two main purposes:

(1) It provides a serial (or application) number and filing date for the application; and

(2) It grants a license to file the application in a foreign country.

After the application is assigned a serial number and filing date, it is passed on to the proper examining group. The Examiner conducts a search and examines the application to see if the invention

PTO-103X
(Rev. 8-95)

FILING RECEIPT

A   B

UNITED STATES DEPARTMENT OF COMMERCE
Patent and Trademark Office
ASSISTANT SECRETARY AND COMMISSIONER
OF PATENTS AND TRADEMARKS
Washington, D.C. 20231

APPLICATION NUMBER	FILING DATE	GRP ART UNIT	FIL FEE REC'D	ATTORNEY DOCKET NO.	DRWGS	TOT CL	IND CL
08/757,302	11/27/96	3504	$425.00	JRD114-1	4	19	4

JOY L BRYANT
703 WHALER DRIVE
NEWPORT NEWS VA 23608

Receipt is acknowledged of this nonprovisional Patent Application. It will be considered in its order and you will be notified as to the results of the examination. Be sure to provide the U.S. APPLICATION NUMBER, FILING DATE, NAME OF APPLICANT, and TITLE OF INVENTION when inquiring about this application. Fees transmitted by check or draft are subject to collection. Please verify the accuracy of the data presented on this receipt. If an error is noted on this Filing Receipt, please write to the Application Processing Division's Customer Correction Branch within 10 days of receipt. Please provide a copy of the Filing Receipt with the changes noted thereon.

Applicant(s)

JOHN R. DIXON III, VIRGINIA BEACH, VA.

C — FOREIGN FILING LICENSE GRANTED 02/04/97   * SMALL ENTITY *
TITLE
INSULATION SUPPORT SYSTEM FOR METAL FRAME CONSTRUCTION AND METHOD
RELATING THERETO

PRELIMINARY CLASS: 052

FIGURE 8.6 *(continues)*

A filing receipt. Section A identifies the application number. Section B gives the application filing date. Section C gives the status of the foreign filing license.

meets the requirements of patentability: novelty, utility, and nonobviousness. The Examiner formulates an opinion regarding the patentability of the invention based on the search results. Typically, this opinion is unfavorable and results in the patent application being rejected. Most patent applications are rejected the first time they are examined, so expect this. The inventor should not construe the rejection in such a way as to think that the patent practitioner did a poor job preparing the application. Rather, the examiner is doing his or

C —— LICENSE FOR FOREIGN FILING UNDER
Title 35, United States Code, Section 184
Title 37, Code of Federal Regulations, 5.11 & 5.15

GRANTED

The applicant has been granted a license under 35 U.S.C. 184, if the phrase "FOREIGN FILING LICENSE GRANTED" followed by a date appears on the reverse side of this form. Such licenses are issued in all applications where the conditions for issuance of a license have been met, regardless of whether or not a license may be required as set forth in 37 CFR 5.11. The scope and limitations of this license are set forth in 37 CFR 5.15(a) unless an earlier license has been issued under 37 CFR 5.15(b). The license is subject to revocation upon written notification. The date indicated is the effective date of the license, unless an earlier license of similar scope has been granted under 37 CFR 5.13 or 5.14.

This license is to be retained by the licensee and may be used at any time on or after the effective date thereof unless it is revoked. This license is automatically transferred to any related application(s) filed under 37 CFR 1.62 which meets the provisions of 37 CFR 5.15(a). This license is not retroactive.

The grant of a license does not in any way lessen the responsibility of a licensee for the security of the subject matter as imposed by any Government contract or the provisions of existing laws relating to espionage and the national security or the export of technical data. Licensees should apprise themselves of current regulations, especially with respect to certain countries, of other agencies, particularly the Office of Defense Trade Controls, Department of State (with respect to Arms, Munitions and Implements of War (22 CFR Parts 121-128)); the Office of Export Administration, Department of Commerce (15 CFR 370.10 (j)); the Office of Foreign Assets Control, Department of Treasury (31 CFR Parts 500+) and the Department of Energy.

NOT GRANTED

No license under 35 U.S.C. 184 has been granted at this time, if the phrase "FOREIGN FILING LICENSE GRANTED" DOES NOT appear on the reverse side of this form. Applicant may still petition for a license under 37 CFR 5.12, if a license is desired before the expiration of 6 months from the fiing date of the application. If 6 months has lapsed from the filing date of this application and the licensee has not received any indication of a secrecy order under 35 U.S.C. 181, the licensee may foreign file the application pursuant to 37 CFR 5.15(b).

FIGURE 8.6 *(continued)*

her job in performing a careful review of the patent application and is shifting the burden of proving that the invention is patentable back to the applicant.

TIP: Expect your patent application to be rejected the first time it is examined.

When the Examiner rejects the patent application, he or she sends an *office action* to the patent practitioner. (This usually takes anywhere from 6 months to 1 year from the time one files the application.) The office action sets forth the reasons why the Examiner rejected the patent application and contains copies of the prior art cited against the patent application. Typically, the patent application is rejected because of a lack of novelty or because the invention is considered obvious in view of the prior art. Figure 8.7 shows the front page of an office action summary. Note that the time to respond to the office action is 3 months from the mailing date. However, extensions of time may be purchased in monthly increments up to 3 months of time, if more time is needed to prepare a response.

When the patent practitioner receives the office action, the inventor is contacted and the office action along with copies of the references cited by the Examiner are sent to the inventor. Most practitioners will explain what needs to be done to overcome the rejection. The practitioner relies on the inventor to provide technical reasons why or how the invention differs from the prior art and combines them with various legal reasons to formulate a response to the office action that will, hopefully, convince the Examiner that the invention is patentable. In some cases, the claims are modified to distinguish the invention from the prior art. These modifications are called *amendments.* In either case no new subject matter may be added to the patent application. In other words, once the application has been filed, the applicant cannot add anything new to it. Therefore, the patent practitioner must rely on what was originally disclosed in the application to get the case allowed.

WARNING: Once a patent application is filed, no new subject matter may be added to it.

Office Action Summary	Application No. 08/757,302	Applicant(s) Dixon	
	Examiner Robert Canfield	Group Art Unit 3504	

A ⎰
⎱

☒ Responsive to communication(s) filed on *Nov 27, 1996* _____ .

☐ This action is **FINAL**.

☐ Since this application is in condition for allowance except for formal matters, prosecution as to the merits is closed in accordance with the practice under *Ex parte Quayle*, 1935 C.D. 11; 453 O.G. 213.

A shortened statutory period for response to this action is set to expire _____ 3 _____ month(s), or thirty days, whichever is longer, from the mailing date of this communication. Failure to respond within the period for response will cause the application to become abandoned. (35 U.S.C. § 133). Extensions of time may be obtained under the provisions of 37 CFR 1.136(a).

Disposition of Claims

B

☒ Claim(s) *1-19* _____ is/are pending in the application.

Of the above, claim(s) _____ is/are withdrawn from consideration.

☐ Claim(s) _____ is/are allowed.

☒ Claim(s) *1-19* _____ is/are rejected.

☐ Claim(s) _____ is/are objected to.

☐ Claims _____ are subject to restriction or election requirement.

Application Papers

☐ See the attached Notice of Draftsperson's Patent Drawing Review, PTO-948.

☐ The drawing(s) filed on _____ is/are objected to by the Examiner.

☐ The proposed drawing correction, filed on _____ is ☐ approved ☐ disapproved.

☐ The specification is objected to by the Examiner.

☐ The oath or declaration is objected to by the Examiner.

Priority under 35 U.S.C. § 119

☐ Acknowledgement is made of a claim for foreign priority under 35 U.S.C. § 119(a)-(d).

☐ All ☐ Some* ☐ None of the CERTIFIED copies of the priority documents have been

☐ received.

☐ received in Application No. (Series Code/Serial Number) _____ .

☐ received in this national stage application from the International Bureau (PCT Rule 17.2(a)).

*Certified copies not received: _____

☐ Acknowledgement is made of a claim for domestic priority under 35 U.S.C. § 119(e).

Attachment(s)

☒ Notice of References Cited, PTO-892

☒ Information Disclosure Statement(s), PTO-1449, Paper No(s). *1 of 1*

☐ Interview Summary, PTO-413

☐ Notice of Draftsperson's Patent Drawing Review, PTO-948

☐ Notice of Informal Patent Application, PTO-152

--- *SEE OFFICE ACTION ON THE FOLLOWING PAGES* ---

U. S. Patent and Trademark Office
PTO-326 (Rev. 9-95)   Office Action Summary   Part of Paper No. __2__

FIGURE 8.7

Front page of an office action. Section A sets the time for responding to the office action. Section B indicates the status of the claims.

The patent practitioner may choose to interview the Examiner at this time. During the interview, issues relating to the patentability of the claims are discussed. The interview is a time when the invention may be more clearly explained to the Examiner and the novel and nonobvious features emphasized. The information gleaned from the interview may be used to amend the claims and/or prepare a response and get the case allowed.

After the practitioner files the amendment or the response to the office action in the U.S.P.T.O., the Examiner reviews it to see if the amendments made distinguish the invention from the prior art. If no amendment has been made, the response is checked to determine whether arguments are presented that are convincing enough to overcome the prior art. If the practitioner is successful in convincing the Examiner, then the application is allowed. However, if the amendment or response is not convincing, the Examiner will reject the application again. Usually, this second rejection is a *final rejection*. At this point, there are four options:

(1) amend the claims one more time;

(2) file an appeal;

(3) refile the patent application, beginning the process again; or

(4) abandon the case.

If the practitioner decides to amend the claims one last time, the Examiner has the option of deciding whether or not he or she will enter the amendment into the case. Thus, there is some risk associated with choosing this option. If the amendment is not entered, the application remains finally rejected and another course of action must be taken.

When the Examiner twice rejects the claims, the applicant may appeal them. An appeal is taken to the Board of Appeals in the U.S.P.T.O. This board consists of three administrative patent judges who hear the case. Usually an appeal is only filed if it is believed that the case may be won based on the appeal.

Refiling the application is another option. If chosen, the claims may be amended or certain claims deleted to overcome the prior art, or the application may be amended to include new subject matter. Applications which are not amended but merely refiled are called *continuations*. When an application has been amended to incorporate new subject matter, it is called a *continuation-in-part*. In either case, the prosecution of the claims begins all over when these types of applications are filed. Another type of application that may be filed is the *continued prosecution application*, which picks up the prosecution where it ended in the first case. Patent practitioners are well versed in this type of practice and will properly advise their clients about what type of application should be filed.

The last option, abandoning the application, is mainly used when there is no way to overcome the prior art. Typically this occurs when a single reference has been found that is identical to the invention. Once an applicant has decided to abandon the application, there is no way to revive it. Therefore, one must give this option serious consideration.

If the Examiner has allowed the patent application, the U.S.P.T.O. will send a notice of allowance and issue fee due. Figure 8.8 shows what the notice looks like. The notice shows the class–subclass for the invention, the small entity status, and indicates how much the issue fee is and when it is due. Note that if the issue fee is not paid by the due date, the application will go abandoned. There is no way to extend this time.

Once the applicant pays the issue fee, the U.S.P.T.O. prints the patent and it issues. Typically, a patent will issue 6 months after the issue fee is paid. To keep the patent enforceable, maintenance fees must be paid by 3.5, 7.5, and 11.5 years from the date the patent is-sues. If the maintenance fee is not paid, the patent is no longer en-forceable. The whole patent process takes approximately 20 months from the time one files the application to the time the patent issues. Figure 8.9 is a flow chart showing the steps in the process and the ap-proximate time involved in getting a patent once the application is filed.

Accelerating the Patent Process

New patent applications are examined in order based on their U.S. filing dates. However, it is possible to have an application exam-ined out of order by filing a *petition to make special.*

> A **petition to make special** is a means for accelerating the patent prosecution process by filing a paper in the U.S.P.T.O. requesting that the case be made special based on certain grounds and, in some instances, paying an ad-ditional fee.

There are 12 different circumstances in which a person may file a petition to make special:[9]

(1) Manufacture—There is written evidence of a prospective U.S. manufacturer with sufficient capital and facilities who is obligat-ed to manufacture the invention immediately upon the allowance of claims or issuance of a patent that protects the invention.

(2) Infringement—A verified statement is provided that al-leges that there is an infringing device or product actually on the market or method in use that infringes the claims in the patent appli-cation.

UNITED STATES DEPARTMENT OF COMMERCE
Patent and Trademark Office

NOTICE OF ALLOWANCE AND ISSUE FEE DUE

CSN1/0116

JOY L. BRYANT
705 WHALER DRIVE
NEWPORT NEWS VA 23608

APPLICATION NO.	FILING DATE	TOTAL CLAIMS	EXAMINER AND GROUP ART UNIT		DATE MAILED
08/908,343	08/07/97	008	BROWN, M	3301	01/16/98

| First Named Applicant | THOMPSON, | JASON A. | | | |

TITLE OF INVENTION BACKBOARD IMMOBILIZATION DEVICE

A   B   C

ATTY'S DOCKET NO.	CLASS-SUBCLASS	BATCH NO.	APPLN. TYPE	SMALL ENTITY	FEE DUE	DATE DUE
3 JATW5-1	128-870.000	W45	UTILITY	YES	$660.00	04/16/98

THE APPLICATION IDENTIFIED ABOVE HAS BEEN EXAMINED AND IS ALLOWED FOR ISSUANCE AS A PATENT.
PROSECUTION ON THE MERITS IS CLOSED.

THE ISSUE FEE MUST BE PAID WITHIN <u>THREE MONTHS</u> FROM THE MAILING DATE OF THIS NOTICE OR THIS APPLICATION SHALL BE REGARDED AS ABANDONED. <u>THIS STATUTORY PERIOD CANNOT BE EXTENDED.</u>

HOW TO RESPOND TO THIS NOTICE:

I. Review the SMALL ENTITY status shown above.
 If the SMALL ENTITY is shown as YES, verify your current SMALL ENTITY status:

  A. If the status is changed, pay twice the amount of the FEE DUE shown above and notify the Patent and Trademark Office of the change in status, or
  B. If the status is the same, pay the FEE DUE shown above.

If the SMALL ENTITY is shown as NO:

  A. Pay FEE DUE shown above, or

  B. File verified statement of Small Entity Status before, or with, payment of 1/2 the FEE DUE shown above.

II. Part B-Issue Fee Transmittal should be completed and returned to the Patent and Trademark Office (PTO) with your ISSUE FEE. Even if the ISSUE FEE has already been paid by charge to deposit account, Part B Issue Fee Transmittal should be completed and returned. If you are charging the ISSUE FEE to your deposit account, section "4b" of Part B-Issue Fee Transmittal should be completed and an extra copy of the form should be submitted.

III. All communications regarding this application must give application number and batch number.
 Please direct all communications prior to issuance to Box ISSUE FEE unless advised to the contrary.

IMPORTANT REMINDER: Utility patents issuing on applications filed on or after Dec. 12, 1980 may require payment of maintenance fees. It is patentee's responsibility to ensure timely payment of maintenance fees when due.

YOUR COPY

PTOL-85 (REV. 10-96) Approved for use through 06/30/99. (0651-0033)

☆U.S. GOVERNMENT PRINTING OFFICE 1997 432-721-52716

FIGURE 8.8

A Notice of Allowance and Issue Fee Due. Section A indicates the small entity status. Section B sets forth the amount of the issue fee and section C states when it is due.

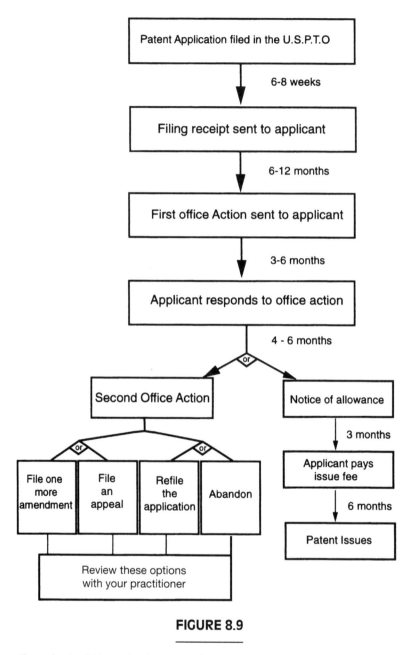

FIGURE 8.9

Flow chart of the patent prosecution process. Note the key events and the time lapse between each event.

(3) Applicant's health—The state of the applicant's health is such that he or she might not be available to assist in the prosecution of the patent application.

(4) Applicant's age—The applicant is 65 years of age or older.

(5) Environmental quality—The invention materially enhances the quality of the environment by contributing to the restoration or maintenance of air, water, and/or soil.

(6) Energy—The invention materially contributes to the discovery or development of energy resources or more efficient use and conservation of energy resources.

(7) Inventions relating to recombinant DNA—For applications relating to safety of research in the field of recombinant DNA.

(8) Special examining procedure for certain new applications—A patent application is submitted having all the claims directed to a single invention, a preexamination search was made and the results submitted to the U.S.P.T.O., along with a detailed discussion of each reference.

(9) Superconductivity—For inventions relating to superconductive materials, their manufacture, and/or application.

(10) Inventions relating to HIV/AIDS and cancer—A verified statement is supplied explaining how the invention contributes to the diagnosis, treatment, or prevention of HIV/AIDS or cancer.

(11) Inventions for countering terrorism—For inventions including systems for detecting/identifying explosives, aircraft sensor/security systems, and vehicular barricades/disabling systems.

(12) Applications relating to biotechnology filed by small entities—For small entities where the subject matter of the patent application is a major asset of the entity and that development of the technology will be significantly impaired if examination of the patent application is delayed.

Most of these petitions require an extra fee besides the patent application filing fee. Exceptions exist for petitions relating to:

(1) Applicant's age;

(2) Applicant's health;

(3) Environmental quality; and

(4) Energy.

These petitions are all filed for free. When the petition is filed, the director of the examining group reviews it. If the group director approves or grants the petition, the Examiner advances the patent application out of turn.

Review

When a patent application is filed, formal papers accompany it. All patent applications are filed with an oath or a declaration by the inventor. Each party associated with the filing and prosecution of a patent application has a duty to disclose to the U.S.P.T.O. all information known to be material to the patentability of the invention in an information disclosure statement. Once a patent application is filed in the U.S.P.T.O., a person may mark the invention "patent pending." Marking an item as patent pending does not provide any exclusive rights in the invention.

When the patent application is examined, the Examiner usually rejects it. The rejection is the Examiner's way of shifting the burden of proving patentability to the applicant. Some form of an amendment or response must be made to the rejection or the application will go abandoned. Most cases are allowed after the Examiner considers the response.

Once the Examiner allows the patent, an issue fee must be paid and the patent issues. To keep the patent enforceable, maintenance fees must be paid. The whole patent process, from the time the application is filed in the U.S.P.T.O. until the patent issues, takes approximately 20 months. Filing a petition to make special may speed up the process depending on the circumstances and the invention.

Annotated References

1. 35 U.S.C. § 115. *(Statutory basis for oath of the applicant.)*
2. Mattor v. Coolegem, 530 F.2d 1391, 189 U.S.P.Q. 201, 204 (C.C.P.A. 1976). *(Precedent for a person following another's instructions is not a coinventor.)*
3. 37 C.F.R. § 1.56. *(Rule regarding duty to disclose information material to patentability.)*
4. Ibid.
5. Ibid.
6. Ibid.
7. Ibid.
8. 35 U.S.C. § 292. *(Statute relating to false marking of patent pending status.)*
9. Manual of Patent Examining Procedure section 708.02. *(Petitions to make special.)*

9

Deciding to Patent

Now that you understand what the patent process is all about, the next step is to decide if if it is a good idea to protect your invention with a patent.

Why Are People Interested in Patenting?

Recently, patents have become a means for creating revenue and a yardstick for measuring performance. Individual inventors seek patent protection to create a source of income for themselves through licensing agreements or to attract venture capital. Academic institutions have turned to creating patent portfolios as a source of generating additional revenue through licensing, as well as a way to attract potential faculty members, and as an indicator demonstrating that state research dollars are being well-invested for the economic benefit of the community. Companies use their patent portfolios to lure potential investors, to assess the value of the corporation, and as a hedge against competitors. The intangible assets created through patents are considered in the valuation process of a company more so now than ever before.[1] Even federal laboratories have joined in by using their patent portfolios as a vehicle for technology transfer. Indeed, the focus is on commercialization of technology through patenting and licensing.

The Cost of Patenting

Patenting is a time consuming and expensive process. The average patent practitioner will take anywhere from 10 to 100 hours to prepare a patent application depending on the technology and the type of patent required. Most patent practitioners charge between $75 and $250 per hour. Therefore, the cost of preparing the patent application may run from as low as $750 to as high as $25,000 depending on the practitioner and the level of technical and legal complexity. The average fee for preparing a patent application is between $4000 and $10,000. In addition, there are prosecution fees or fees for preparing responses to office actions. These fees usually start at $1000.

The practitioner's fees do not include the patent office user fees. The U.S. Patent and Trademark Office (U.S.P.T.O.) operates based on these fees. Consequently, there are very few papers that may be sent to the U.S.P.T.O. without having a check accompany them. The patent office user fees are assessed based on the applicant's status as a large entity or a small entity. Small entities receive a 50% reduction for most of the fees.

The Cost of Patenting

Table 9.1 provides a partial listing of the patent office user fees as of October 1997. The U.S.P.T.O. has raised these fees by 3% each year for the past several years. Therefore, the fees shown are only reliable through September 1998. Referring to the table, the patent office user fees associated with getting a utility patent may be calculated. Assume that the calculation is for a small entity and that the invention is not going to be assigned. Also, assume that the patent ap-

TABLE 9.1

Selected Patent Office User Fees[a]

Description	Large entity	Small entity
Filing a Disclosure Document	$10.00	$10.00
Provisional Patent Application filing fee	$150.00	$75.00
Utility Patent Application filing fee, 20 claims, 3 independent claims	$790.00	$395.00
Design Patent Application filing fee	$330.00	$165.00
Plant Patent Application filing fee	$540.00	$270.00
Independent claims in excess of three (per claim)	$82.00	$41.00
Claims in excess of twenty (per claim)	$22.00	$11.00
Multiple dependent claim (per claim)	$270.00	$135.00
Utility Patent Issue fee	$1320.00	$660.00
Design Patent Issue fee	$450.00	$225.00
Plant Patent Issue fee	$670.00	$335.00
Maintenance fee due at 3.5 years	$1050.00	$525.00
Maintenance fee due at 7.5 years	$2100.00	$1050.00
Maintenance fee due at 11.5 years	$3160.00	$1580.00
One month extension of time	$110.00	$55.00
Two month extension of time	$400.00	$200.00
Three month extension of time	$950.00	$475.00
Four month extension of time	$1510.00	$755.00
Five month extension of time	$2060.00	$1030.00
Notice of Appeal	$310.00	$155.00
Filing a brief in support of an appeal	$310.00	$155.00
Assignment recordal fee	$40.00	$40.00

[a]As of October 1997. Fees subject to change.

plication only has a total of 20 claims, 3 of which are independent, and that there are no other prosecution fees, such as extensions of time or appeals. (This is the lowest cost scenario.) The patent office user fees are calculated as follows:

Utility filing fee:	$395
Utility issue fee:	660
Total	$1055

Thus, if a utility patent application is filed having 20 claims, 3 of which are independent, and small entity status is claimed, the minimum U.S.P.T.O. user fee is $1055.00. This fee is paid in addition to the practitioner's fees. In general, one should expect to pay between $10,000 and $25,000 to get a patent depending on the technology and its level of complexity. Because of the costs involved, the decision to patent must be made carefully. This decision should not be based solely on cost but should also take into consideration various factors relating to commercializing the technology.

Making Money with a Patent

Many people think that simply because they have a patent, they will make money. This is not true. An invention, whether patented or not, will not make any money if it is not commercialized. Therefore, in order to make money, based on patenting, one must get the product to market or commercialize it. An individual has three main options with respect to commercialization:

(1) establish a company to manufacture and sell the invention;

(2) sell the patent outright; or

(3) license the patent.

MANUFACTURING AND SELLING
THE INVENTION

The decision to manufacture and sell the invention is risky and places the inventor in business in the true sense of the word. The main risk incurred is the capital investment that must be made to establish the company. Despite this risk, if the invention is a commercial success, the inventor will more likely make more money than he or she would from selling or licensing the patent. However, before going through the expense of patenting and manufacturing the invention, the technical, marketing, and legal strengths of the invention need to be considered. In particular, with respect to the legal strengths of the invention the following questions should be considered.

(1) What type of impact will the invention have on the marketplace?

(2) Does the invention infringe on someone else's patent?

(3) What scope of claim protection is obtainable?

(4) Is the patent enforceable?

The novel or patentable feature(s) of the invention should be assessed to determine its value to a particular user. For example, if the patentable feature offers some advantage over an existing product currently on the market and consumers prefer it, then there is value in the invention. The consumer preference for the patented invention offers the patentee an opportunity to gain market share and possibly higher profit margins if the patented feature is such that consumers are willing to pay more for it. These higher profit margins help to justify protecting the invention with a patent and will offset the costs of patenting.

Another factor to consider is the life of the product. If the invention is such that it is a "fad" item or something that will quickly become obsolete such as a computer software program, then patenting may not be a viable option. Remember, the average pendency for a patent application is about 20 months. Therefore, if the product has a limited shelf-life of 3 years or less, patenting may not be a wise choice. However, if there are patentable features of the invention that do not have a limited shelf life, patent protection should be sought.

There are advantages to patenting an invention despite its limited consumer value or short shelf-life. These advantages are associated with marketing the invention. If a patent is pending or has issued, the product may be marked either "patent pending" or with the patent number (it is illegal to mark a product "patent pending" if there is no patent pending). Marking the product helps emphasize its uniqueness in the marketplace, encouraging consumers to purchase it.

Before a product is placed on the market, a market clearance should be obtained. A market clearance is typically granted by a patent attorney who conducts a study and renders an opinion. The clearance takes into consideration competitive patents that have issued. These patents are reviewed to determine whether the product infringes on a patent (or patents) or whether there is a dominating patent that would prevent practicing the invention. If there is a dominating patent, the product must be redesigned to get around the existing patents, a licensing agreement must be made, or the project must be terminated.

EXAMPLE

XYZ company owns a patent claiming a voice-activated switch. Rob, an independent inventor, improved the voice-activated switch but used several components protected by XYZ's patent. Rob was able to obtain a patent for his invention but his patent fell within the scope of the claims for XYZ's patent. Therefore, in order for Rob to make, use or sell his switch without triggering a lawsuit from XYZ company, he must get permission from XYZ company to use their patented components.

Another factor to consider in deciding to patent is the claim scope. Remember, the claims define the legal limits of protection for the invention. If the prior art is such that the claim scope for the invention is narrow and easy to design around, deciding to seek patent protection may not be wise. However, if the various design alternatives are patentable, a strategic move would be to build a portfolio of patents based on the different designs of a particular invention. When broad claim coverage is obtainable and the marketing factors are favorable, patent protection should be sought.

The last item to consider with respect to patenting is enforcement. In order to prevent competitors from making, using, selling, and importing the invention in the U.S., the patent must be enforced by the patentee. Therefore, the nature of the invention must be considered when deciding to patent. In particular, process patents may or may not be difficult to enforce. For example, if the invention is for a process that yields a product that is unique to the process, then enforcing the patent will be possible by looking at the final product. However, if the process does not yield a unique product, detecting which process is being used to make the product and enforcing the patent will be difficult.

Patent enforcement entails bringing a lawsuit upon the infringer. The costs associated with patent litigation begin at around $250,000[2] and can run into millions of dollars. Most individuals, small start-up companies, and academic institutions cannot afford this. Recently, insurance companies have recognized this and have started to address the problem by offering patent infringement insurance that will cover the legal costs associated with a patent infringement suit (either offensive or defensive).[3] However, if the net sales of the patented product are more than $250,000 per year, the cost of enforcing the patent is less of an issue.

SELLING THE PATENT

Selling one's rights in a patent is perhaps the quickest way to make money from the patent process. To sell the patent, one assigns or transfers the rights in the patent to another party in exchange for an agreed-upon sum of money. The assignment transfers the ownership from the inventor to another party. For most inventors in a corporate environment, this is typically done through an employment agreement where the inventor agrees to assign the rights in the invention to the company in exchange for a salary and other considerations depending on the company. In turn, the company holds the rights in the patent and incurs the responsibility of commercializing the technology and enforcing the patent.

If an independent inventor patents a product that is within the scope of a particular corporation's business interests, the inventor may choose to assign the patent to the company in exchange for one lump-sum payment (which may not be in the inventor's best interest). However, the difficulty for an individual inventor comes in identifying the company and "getting in the door". Most companies in the U.S. prefer to conduct business with those they know. Therefore, cold-calling a company and offering a patent for sale often results in limited to no success. An individual inventor should realize that getting in the door of a particular company may not be as easy as it sounds. In order to be successful, it may be necessary to have the corporate contact before trying to sell the invention. Therefore, if the plan is to patent and assign the invention to a company, be sure that:

(1) you have the company contacts to achieve this;

(2) the company is interested in what you have to offer; or

(3) you consult with a legitimate licensing executive or technology transfer firm.[4]

LICENSING A PATENT

Licensing is the main vehicle for technology transfer. It is used by industry, individuals, academic institutions, and federal laboratories.

> A **patent license** is a contractual grant of permission to use a particular patented technology for a defined time, context, market line, or territory.

Licensing differs from assignment in that the title to the patent is not transferred. Instead, the patent owner (licensor) negotiates with another party (licensee) to allow the licensee to use the patented technology in exchange for a royalty. A royalty is a negotiated or prenegotiated sum of money, typically based on the sales of the invention, that is incrementally paid to the patent owner by a licensee in exchange for the right to make, use, sell, or import the patented technology. A license, simply put, is an agreement that the licensor will not sue the licensee for patent infringement.

Licensing typically involves an up-front fee and often an incremental royalty payment to the patent owner. The up-front fee is usually a lump sum to cover the costs of patenting and initial research and development costs. The royalty rate is determined based on the industry. Typical royalty rates range from 0.25% to 10% (or more) of the selling price of the product depending on the:

(1) technology strength;

(2) market;

(3) legal aspects of the invention; and

(4) type of license.

There are essentially two types of licenses that may be granted:

(1) nonexclusive licenses and

(2) exclusive licenses.

A nonexclusive license is a grant to more than one entity of the right to use the patented technology within some scope or field defined by the license. Usually, a lower royalty rate is charged for nonexclusive licenses. Conversely, exclusive licenses usually command a higher royalty rate, are granted to one particular entity or licensee, and are defined by the license based on:

(1) a particular scope, such as a product line;

(2) a specific field of use;

(3) a territory; or

(4) a certain amount of time.

When an exclusive license is granted, the patent owner (licensor) promises the licensee that others will not be granted licenses of the same rights as those given to the licensee.

As with selling the patent, an inventor faces the challenge of locating a potential licensee. Academic institutions and federal laboratories have success with overcoming this challenge because often the patentable technology results from a research project that was conducted with an industrial partner. Individual inventors may not have this advantage so they are challenged with having to locate potential licensees. This requires time, effort and money in addition to the costs of patenting. However, if the inventor is successful, he or she can look forward to enjoying the rewards of the royalty income.

Unlike assignment, in licensing, the ownership of the patent is not transferred. Therefore, the responsibility of patent enforcement rests with the patent owner. Licensing a patent or granting a party an exclusive license does not relieve the owner of the patent from the responsibility to enforce it. However, the licensee may *join* the licensor in enforcing the patent against infringers.

Preventing Others from Getting a Patent

If the decision is made not to patent an invention, there are several ways to prevent others from patenting the technology. This is possible by creating a statutory bar. As discussed in Chapter 3, statutory bars will prohibit patenting in the U.S. Therefore, by creating a statutory bar, competitors will be forced to quickly file a patent application before the 1-year grace period expires.

One effective low-cost way to create a statutory bar is through publication of the invention. Simply publishing the invention in a journal,[5] newspaper, or on the Internet will start the 1-year grace period in which a person must file a patent application. Also, it is likely that the publication will be cited against the patent application when it is examined, forcing the applicant to either argue over the reference or show a date of invention prior to the date of the reference. This will be difficult if the applicant is not the original inventor.

Another way to create a statutory bar is to offer the invention for sale or publicly use the invention. This is easily achieved by placing the invention on display at a trade show or distributing brochures offering the invention for sale. In the past, different government agencies were very efficient at triggering this statutory bar. With the focus on technology transfer, several government agencies were known for hosting trade shows that solicited potential industrial partners to enter into possible licensing agreements with that agency. Recently, this practice has declined.

The last way to invoke a statutory bar involves the filing of a *statutory invention registration* (SIR). A statutory invention registration is a type of defensive patent. Instead of granting an exclusive right to the inventor, it prevents others from being able to obtain a patent for the same invention. In essence, the inventor waives his or her right to enforce the patent but enjoys the benefits of having the SIR serve as a prior art reference. It is classified, cross-referenced, and placed into the U.S.P.T.O. and foreign search files.

> A **statutory invention registration** is a patent-like document by which an inventor may officially and affirmatively put the invention into the public domain for defensive purposes.[6]

Because a SIR is a patent-like document, it involves and requires the formal preparation of a patent application. In addition, the patent application must be filed in the U.S.P.T.O. and the filing fee must be paid. The patent application is converted to a SIR anytime after it is filed. The cost of doing this is $920 minus the initial filing fee if the application has not yet been examined. If the application has been examined, the fee for converting the application to a SIR is $1840 minus the initial filing fee. Note, SIRs are rare and most people opt to publish their inventions in newspapers or journals which do not have the associated costs.

Review

The advantage to patenting is that it provides the owner with the right to exclude others from making, using, selling or importing the invention in the U.S. Without a patent, one must face the competition head-on. For a product with a short shelf-life, this may not be so bad. However, for those products having a shelf-life greater than 3 years, the competition could defeat a business.

For those entities who wish to create a revenue stream through the payment of royalties, patent protection may be the only option. Patents secure the property rights in the invention and serve as a vehicle for licensing new technology. The real advantage to having a patent for an invention resides in the exclusive rights granted to the patentee (Figure 9.1).

Annotated References

1. Edvinsson, Leif and Michael S. Malone (1997). *In* "Intellectual Capital". HarperCollins Publishers, Inc., New York. *(Resource for information about valuing a company based on its intellectual capital.)*

2. Private communication with Anthony Venturino, Esq. of Stevens, Davis, Miller & Mosher, L.L.P., Washington, D.C. *(Cost of patent litigation.)*

3. Intellectual Property Insurance Services Corporation, Louisville, Kentucky. *(Company offering intellectual property insurance.)*

4. First Principals, Inc., Cleveland, Ohio. *(A firm specializing in technology transfer and commercialization.)*

5. "Research Disclosure," Kenneth Mason Publications, Ltd., U.K. *(A defensive publication that prevents others from patenting similar technologies while minimizing costs and eliminating the need to obtain a patent.)*

6. McCarthy, J. T. (1996). *In* "McCarthy's Desk Encyclopedia of Intellectual Property" 2nd ed., pp. 415–416. BNA Books, Washington, DC. *(Definition of statutory invention registration.)*

The Commissioner of
Patents and Trademarks

Has received an application for a patent for a new and useful invention. The title and description of the invention are enclosed. The requirements of law have been complied with, and it has been determined that a patent on the invention shall be granted under the law.

Therefore, this

United States Patent

Grants to the person(s) having title to this patent the right to exclude others from making, using, offering for sale, or selling the invention throughout the United States of America or importing the invention into the United States of America for the term set forth below, subject to the payment of maintenance fees as provided by law.

If this application was filed prior to June 8, 1995, the term of this patent is the longer of seventeen years from the date of grant of this patent or twenty years from the earliest effective U.S. filing date of the application, subject to any statutory extension.

If this application was filed on or after June 8, 1995, the term of this patent is twenty years from the U.S. filing date, subject to any statutory extension. If the application contains a specific reference to an earlier filed application or applications under 35 U.S.C. 120, 121 or 365(c), the term of the patent is twenty years from the date on which the earliest application was filed, subject to any statutory extension.

Bruce Lehman

Commissioner of Patents and Trademarks

Melvinia Gary

Attest

FIGURE 9.1

The ribboned page from a U.S. utility patent. This page is only available to the patentee. The seal is gold foil and the ribbon is red. Note that the page sets forth, in writing, a grant from the Commissioner of Patents and Trademarks the right to exclude others from making, using, offering for sale, or selling the invention throughout the U.S. or importing the invention into the U.S. for a specific term.

Resources

Organization	Address	Phone number	Web address	Description
U.S. Copyright Office	Copyright Office Library of Congress 101 Independence Ave., S.E., Washington, DC 20559	(202) 707-3000 (info. line) (202) 707-9100 (forms)	http://lcweb.loc.gov/copyright/	Provide information and forms for obtaining U.S. copyrights.
U.S. Patent and Trademark Office	Assistant Commissioner for Trademarks 2900 Crystal Drive Arlington, VA 22202-3513	(703) 308-4357	http://www.uspto.gov	Provide information relating to trademarks..
U.S. Patent and Trademark Office	Assistant Commissioner for Patents Washington, DC 20231	(800) 786-9199	http://www.uspto.gov	Provide information relating to patents.
U.S.P.T.O. Office of Enrollment and Discipline	Box OED Assistant Commissioner for Patents Washington, DC 20231	(703) 308-5278	http://www.uspto.gov	Provide information regarding patent practitioner standing in the U.S.P.T.O.

National Association of Patent Practitioners	435-2 Oriana Road, Suite 215 Newport News, VA 23608	(800) 216-9588	http://www.napp.org	Provide membership roster listing patent practitioners by area of expertise
U.S.P.T.O. Public Search Room	Crystal Plaza 3, 1A01 2021 Jefferson Davis Highway Arlington, VA	(800) 786-9199	http://www.uspto.gov	U.S.P.T.O. public search room. Open 8 AM – 8 PM, Monday–Friday, except federal holidays.
Scientific Notebook Company	P.O. Box 238 Stevensville, MI 49127	(616) 429-8285 (800) 537-3028	http://www.snco.com/	Source for bound laboratory notebooks.
First Principals, Inc.	4440 Warrensville Center Road Suite 1000 Cleveland, OH 44128	(216) 586-6332	http://www.firstprincipals.com	Technology transfer and commercialization.

APPENDIX

Patent and Trademark Depository Libraries[a]

.

State	City	Location/name of library	Telephone number
Alabama	Auburn	Auburn University	(334) 844-1747
	Birmingham	Birmingham Public Library	(205) 226-3620
Alaska	Anchorage	Anchorage Municipal Libraries	(907) 562-7323
Arizona	Tempe	Arizona State University	(602) 965-7010
Arkansas	Little Rock	Arkansas State Library	(501) 682-2053
California	Los Angeles	Los Angeles Public Library	(213) 228-7220
	Sacramento	California State Library	(916) 654-0069
	San Diego	San Diego Public Library	(619) 236-5813
	San Francisco	San Francisco Public Library	(415) 557-4500
	Sunnyvale	Sunnyvale Center for Innovation	(408) 730-7290

State	City	Location/name of library	Telephone number
Colorado	Denver	Denver Public Library	(303) 640-6220
Connecticut	None		
Delaware	Newark	University of Delaware Library	(302) 831-2965
District of Columbia	Washington	Howard University	(202) 806-7252
Florida	Fort Lauderdale	Broward County Main Library	(954) 357-7444
	Miami	Miami-Dade Public Library	(305) 375-2665
	Orlando	University of Central Florida	(407) 823-2562
	Tampa	University of South Florida	(813) 974-2726
Georgia	Atlanta	Georgia Institute of Technology	(404) 894-4508
Hawaii	Honolulu	Hawaii State Library	(808) 586-3477
Idaho	Moscow	University of Idaho Library	(208) 885-6235
Illinois	Chicago	Chicago Public Library	(312) 747-4450
	Springfield	Illinois State Library	(217) 782-5659
Indiana	Indianapolis	Indianapolis-Marion County Public Library	(317) 269-1741
	West Lafayette	Purdue University	(317) 494-2872
Iowa	Des Moines	State Library of Iowa	(515) 281-4118
Kansas	Wichita	Wichita State University	(316) 978-3155
Kentucky	Louisville	Louisville Free Public Library	(502) 574-1611
Louisiana	Baton Rouge	Louisiana State University	(504) 388-8875
Maine	Orono	University of Maine	(207) 581-1678
Maryland	College Park	University of Maryland	(301) 405-9157
Massachusetts	Amherst	University of Massachusetts	(413) 545-1370
	Boston	Boston Public Library	(617) 536-5400
Michigan	Ann Arbor	University of Michigan	(313) 647-5735
	Big Rapids	Ferris State University	(616) 592-3602
	Detroit	Detroit Public Library	(313) 833-3379
Minnesota	Minneapolis	Minneapolis Public Library	(612) 372-6570
Mississippi	Jackson	Mississippi Library Commission	(601) 359-1036
Missouri	Kansas City	Linda Hall Library	(816) 363-4600
	St. Louis	St. Louis Public Library	(314) 241-2288

State	City	Location/name of library	Telephone number
Montana	Butte	University of Montana	(406) 496-4281
Nebraska	Lincoln	Engineering Library, Nebraska Hall, 2nd Floor West	(402) 472-3411
Nevada	Reno	University of Nevada-Reno	(702) 784-6500
New Hampshire	Concord	New Hampshire State Library	(603) 271-2239
New Jersey	Newark	Newark Public Library	(201) 733-7782
	Piscataway	Rutgers University	(908) 445-2895
New Mexico	Albuquerque	University of New Mexico	(505) 277-4412
New York	Albany	New York State Library	(518) 474-5355
	Buffalo	Buffalo & Erie County Public Library	(716) 858-7101
	New York	Science, Industry & Business Library	(212) 592-7000
North Carolina	Raleigh	North Carolina State University	(919) 515-3280
North Dakota	Grand Forks	University of North Dakota	(701) 777-4888
Ohio	Akron	Akron-Summit County Public Library	(330) 643-9075
	Cincinnati	Public Library of Cincinnati & Hamilton County	(513) 369-6936
	Cleveland	Cleveland Public Library	(216) 623-2870
	Columbus	Ohio State University	(614) 292-6175
	Toledo	Toledo/Lucas County Public Library	(419) 259-5212
Oklahoma	Stillwater	Oklahoma State University	(405) 744-7086
Oregon	Portland	Lewis & Clark College	(503) 768-6786
Pennsylvania	Philadelphia	The Free Library of Philadelphia	(215) 686-5331
	Pittsburgh	Carnegie Library of Pittsburgh	(412) 622-3138
	University Park	Pennsylvania State University	(814) 865-4861
Puerto Rico	Mayaguez	University of Puerto Rico	(787) 832-4040
Rhode Island	Providence	Providence Public Library	(401) 455-8027
South Carolina	Clemson	Clemson University	(864) 656-3024

(continued on next page)

State	City	Location/name of library	Telephone number
South Dakota	Rapid City	South Dakota School of Mines & Technology	(605) 394-6822
Tennessee	Memphis	Memphis & Shelby County Public Library	(901) 725-8877
	Nashville	Vanderbilt University	(615) 322-2717
Texas	Austin	University of Texas at Austin	(512) 495-4500
	College Station	Texas A&M University	(409) 845-3826`
	Dallas	Dallas Public Library	(214) 670-1468
	Houston	Rice University	(713) 527-8101
	Lubbock	Texas Tech University	(806) 742-2282
Utah	Salt Lake City	University of Utah	(801) 581-8394
Vermont	Burlington	University of Vermont	(802) 656-2542
Virginia	Richmond	Virginia Commonwealth University	(804) 828-1104
Washington	Seattle	University of Washington	(206) 543-0740
West Virginia	Morgantown	West Virginia University	(304) 293-2510
Wisconsin	Madison	University of Wisconsin-Madison	(608) 262-6845
	Milwaukee	Milwaukee Public Library	(414) 286-3051
Wyoming	Casper	Natrona County Public Library	(307) 237-4935

[a]As of January 1998.

Tips Regarding Invention Development Firms

1. Ask for the total cost of the firm's services from researching the invention through marketing and licensing the invention. If you cannot get a straight answer, walk away.

2. If the fee for invention assistance or marketing services is greater than $5000, walk away.

3. Ask the firm to disclose its success rate along with names and telephone numbers of recently successful clients. Be leery of a success rate that is greater than 25%. Call the people on the list.

4. Ask the firm what percentage of inventions they find unacceptable. If the percentage is less than 75%, walk away.

5. Do not pay more than $10 to file a Disclosure Document in the U.S.P.T.O.

6. Be leery of the firm that agrees to identify manufacturers by coding your idea with the U.S. Bureau of Standard Industrial Code (SIC). These lists are of limited value.

7. Question claims and assurances that your invention will make money.

8. Call the Better Business Bureau, the consumer protection agency, and the Attorney General in your city or state, and in the city or state where the firm is located to find out if there are any unresolved consumer complaints about the firm.

9. Make sure your contract contains the terms you agreed to before you sign. Have your attorney review the contract.

APPENDIX

IV

What the Patent Practitioner Needs

1. Names, addresses, and countries of citizenship for all the people involved with the invention

2. Title for the invention

3. For federally funded research, name of the agency and grant number

4. List of dates when any of the following events occurred:

    (a) invention first displayed in public

    (b) invention first described in a publication

    (c) invention described orally at a public meeting

    (d) intent to publish the invention within the next 6 months

    (e) invention offered for sale

(f) invention revealed to a third party and whether a nondisclosure agreement was used (copy of signed nondisclosure agreement)

5. Description of the technical area of classification for the invention

6. Description of the problem(s) solved by the invention and how others failed at solving the problem(s)

7. Brief description (25 words or less) how the invention solves the problem(s) described in point 6

8. Drawing(s) showing each physical or functional element of the invention

9. Possible variations to the invention

10. Structural/functional differences between the invention and the prior references

11. Reasons why the solution to the problem would not be apparent to others working on the same problem

12. Step-by-step instructions on how to make the invention

13. List of possible uses for the invention

14. Laboratory notebook and other documentation relating to the invention

Index

royalty free
Rules for good record keeping, *see*
    Record keeping, rules

Scope, *see* Claims, scope
Search firms, professional, 101
Search room, public, 101
Search
    assignee name, 106
    examining group, 101
    field of, 103
    Internet, 98
        sites, 99
    inventor name, 105
    keyword, 101, 102
    literature, 98
        conducting, 97
    manual, 101
    patentability, 64
    preliminary, 63
Secret prior art, *see* Prior art, secret
Senior party, *see* Interference, senior
        party
Service mark, definition of, 16
Services, commercial online, 100
Sexually reproduced plants, *see*
        Plants, sexually reproduced
SIR, *see* Statutory invention
        registration
Slogans, 8
Small business concern, 167
Small entity
    definition of, 164
    statement, 164
Sole inventor, *see* Inventor, sole
Specification, 50
    definition of, 142
    enabling, 51, 143, 145
    requirements, 142–143

Statute of Monopolies, 5
Statutory bar, 109, 172, 197
    definition, of 92
Statutory invention registration, 198
Summary of the invention, *see*
        Invention, summary of

Technical literature, *see* Literature,
        technical
Technology transfer, 188
Theses, *see* Publication, theses
Time, extension, 63, 176
Title, *see* Invention, title
Townsend-Pernell Plant Patent Act,
        57
Trade catalogs, *see* Publication, trade
        catalogs
Trade name, definition of, 16
Trade secret, 20–23, 113
    definition of, 3
    disclosure of, 22
    information protected, 20
    maintaining, 21
    requirements to obtain protection,
        21
    term, 23
    theft, 88
Trademark, 15–20
    application of, 15
    applying for, 17
    constitutional basis, 6
    definition of, 2
    federally registered, 17
    function, 15
    intent-to-use application, 18
    Internet, 19, 20
    registration renewal, 20
    requirements for registration, 18
    state registered, 17

ISBN 0-12-138410-1

90066